Inspiring Voices books may be ordered through booksellers or by contacting:

Inspiring Voices
1663 Liberty Drive
Bloomington, IN 47403
www.inspiringvoices.com
1-(866) 697-5313

Cover by Müllerhaus
Certain stock imagery © Thinkstock.
Interior photos by Luanne Bandy Holzloehner and Mike Frezon

ISBN: 978-1-4624-0077-5 (sc)
ISBN: 978-1-4624-0076-8 (e)

Library of Congress Control Number: 2012934096

Printed in the United States of America

Inspiring Voices rev. date: 03/05/2012
10 9 8 7 6 5 4 3 2

Heart to Heart, Hand in Paw

How One Woman Finds
Faith and Hope through the
Healing Love of Animals

Peggy Frezon

Guideposts

New York

Acknowledgments

Thank you to David, Carl, Alan, Amanda, Sandy and everyone at Inspiring Voices. To my family for their love and support, and to my always-inspiring Guideposts family. A special thanks to Kate Fenner, Shawnelle Eliasen and Patricia Punt.

SDG

Dedication

To Mom, who loves all creatures great and small.

Author's Note

The stray dog cowered on our doorstep. He was skinny, wet and smelly, and I couldn't wait to throw my arms around him. His soft, mocha eyes remained gentle when I touched him. That single moment—hugging a homely, abandoned dog—launched my lifelong love of animals.

But this isn't my story. It's my mother's story. She was there first, accepting the stray dog, stroking his muddy back. Checking his paws for wounds. It's her story of hardships and courage, but most of all, hope. It's about Luanne and the many different animals she's loved, and how they loved her back. The stray dogs, the chickens and goats, the rejected lamb.

As with most true stories, the pieces are put together through personal experiences, interviews, research, and best guesses to fill in the gaps. I visited her farm, met her animals, and witnessed her way of life. I grew up listening to the stories of her childhood, of Upchuck the beagle and Toy the parrot. Together we laughed and cried as she shared these stories. They are recalled to the best of her ability and recorded to the best of my ability.

Her experiences remind me to be grateful for the roof over my head, the pets under my roof, and for healing bonds between humans and animals.

Contents

ANIMALS LOVE

Animals Heal

Chapter 1

Blown Away, Literally

EARLIER THAT MORNING, she'd had a home. But now, all that was left on the property was a dog.

Luanne could see him sitting there all alone as her husband urged the old station wagon up the grassy hill with no driveway. A fall storm mighty enough to rip the sheets off the line had kicked up and the blue nylon pup tent they'd been living in was gone. Luanne thought about that for a moment, but when you've been through a lot, a tent seemed insignificant. In truth, she was more concerned about the dog.

The winds that had relocated their living quarters had also erased any trace of dignity in the dog's appearance. His dense, curly fur, its coloring donated from every breed seen 'round the back roads, plastered against his body. Lingering gusts brushed a few loose strands of fur across his eyes. His long, knobby-kneed legs bulged at the bottom like an old lady whose stockings had fallen down. One ear folded inside out, and his tongue lolled to the side. He shook, sending wet droplets flying. He'd watched the world bluster by and now just sat there as if he had nothing to do and no place to go. Luanne didn't even wait for Henry to ease the car to a stop before flinging open the passenger door, leaning out and spreading her arms wide. "You didn't blow away!"

Corky, by no means a lap dog, bolted into the car, jumped on top of her, and embraced her with his paws. His drenched body soaked her shirt. Just as she didn't mind that he was bedraggled and soggy, she knew that the dog didn't care what she looked like. Surely she was far from the most beautiful woman ever to set down a bowl of dog food. It didn't matter to him that her legs were short and her hair was plain old brown. He certainly didn't notice her department store sweatshirts and no-name tennis shoes. As long as they were together, he was happy. She pulled him to her. "I got to you as fast as I could," she said.

Throughout the afternoon she'd anxiously watched the rain pelt against the classroom windows where she worked as an aide for special needs kids, and worried about getting home to check on Corky. Some of the students had reacted to the storm too, shuddering at each abrupt burst of thunder. Others seemed to barely notice, attracted instead to the tank of goldfish on the back counter. Luanne had acquired the fish from her daughter, who was unable to take the heavy tank with her to college. Lucky that the class welcomed the aquatic addition. An aquarium certainly wouldn't have fit in the tent!

Now, with the tent blown away, there wasn't even a place for Luanne and Henry—and Corky—to stay. This wasn't the way they'd planned things! They were newlyweds, although she was in her forties and he was in his fifties. A second marriage for each. With all the kids except her youngest son Randy grown up and on their own, they'd each put their houses up for sale and bought a piece of land in the country. When the houses sold faster than expected, however, they were left with a piece of land and dreams. Dreams of building their own log home, dreams of living off the land. Dreams, as often is the case, that were larger than their pocketbooks, more demanding than their potential energy and certainly more ambitious than any common sense.

A few sweatshirts and a work boot trailed across the grassy field, indicating the direction the wind had taken their wayward dwelling. "It could have blown fifty miles away by now," Luanne said.

"Easy come, easy go," Henry reasoned. His Vermont practicality showed. She knew that not even the sight of the empty lot threw him. It happened. He pulled his plaid flannel shirt tighter around his neck and scratched his chin. "Guess I should take a look for it."

Luanne stayed put but her mind raced to make plans. Could they stay with friends? What about Randy; he'd just started his sophomore year of high school there. Where would he stay? Could they replace what they'd lost? She let out a jagged breath and rubbed the dog's damp neck. He sank into her, resting his head on her shoulder. Her breathing began to steady. Everything would all be okay. After all, they still had each other. And the land.

When she and Henry had first set sights on the rugged five acres situated an hour's drive from the city, they weren't impressed. A dirt road led them miles away from the nearest community, miles even from the lone general store with the bags of grain stacked out front. Twists and turns in the narrow bumpy lane, potholed from mud season, wound up a sharp wooded grade. She'd wondered if anyone but bears lived out that far.

The building lot was steep as well. The land had once been part of a gravel pit. It looked almost as if a big bite had been taken out of the bottom of the land, with a wide ledge at the top. She and Henry hadn't even ventured farther than the roadside at the base of the hill, looking up and shaking their heads. Who in their right mind would build a home there? Inexplicably, the property never left her mind.

She imagined great potential; the log house they planned to build. The gardens. And most of all, the animals. Animals like the ones that had followed her and saved her all of her life. Animals who had been more like family to her than actual relatives. Animals who had comforted her when she felt neglected, eased her childhood loneliness, and stood by her through divorce and hard times. God had put these animals in her life for a purpose. Without them, she'd never have survived—of that she was sure.

A few weeks after the initial visit to the property, she and Henry returned with Randy. He'd have to deal with this, to live every day with their choices. At least until he was off and on his own. "Think you could live here?" she'd asked softly. Maybe he wouldn't see this as the same exciting adventure she did. He'd have to change schools, make new friends. Rough it in close quarters and rustic conditions. Pitch in to help build the house. Maybe that sounded like the worst kind of punishment to a teenager. He might even take off and go live with his father. She'd swallowed hard. Maybe she'd lose him.

Randy had stretched his long legs in the back seat of the car and looked out the window at the dirt and weeds. She was certain he'd change his mind right then and there, but he smiled and said, "Why not?"

"Yes? Really?" She beamed at him, proud that maybe he did share their vision. "Okay, then, let's drive up and take a closer look." They bumped over what would have been the driveway, had there been one. Small wonder they didn't get stuck along the way. When they reached the top and climbed out, everyone stared first at their feet and the pebbly dirt, then across the weed-laden fields, and then, at last, up to the countryside surrounding them. That's when they all fell silent.

From below she had seen nothing but overgrown grass bordered by stands of pines and maple trees. From above, however, the view spread out to a sweeping vista that made her feel as wondrous as if she were before Michelangelo's masterpiece at the Sistine Chapel. She couldn't stop staring at the panorama of the distant Green Mountains in all their majestic fall glory. The gentle chain seemed to have no beginning and no end.

She'd never felt more free. The immense sky was painted a delicate blue with warm rays of sun shimmering down. And the mountains! They breathed with every shade of red, orange and yellow imaginable. This was a sight she could wake up and see every morning and be happy.

So, as impulsively as they'd conceived the plan of living off the land, they'd bought the property with all its imperfections but also with the glorious view that would make up for it all. And now, even through the filmy fog and rain from the storm that had blown away the tent, Luanne still felt awed by the mountains' power.

"I found it!" Henry called from over a bank at the edge of the woods. He lofted a tattered wad of nylon and a bent pole. "Well, part of it."

"That's certainly not livable. What do we do now?" She'd need to make temporary arrangements for themselves, Randy and Corky. And work on the house would be delayed. She closed her eyes and tried to picture the dream. The land with their very own log home. The farm. A place where she would surround herself with animals of every size and shape. Abandoned dogs. Unwanted cats. She'd take them all. Maybe if she'd had a consistent home of her own, she wouldn't have cared so much about the homelessness of others. If she'd had an easy life, she might not have picked up on their suffering. But she'd been abandoned, unwanted, unloved. Deep inside, she was afraid it was true—that she wasn't good enough. But then there were the animals. Cats, dogs, birds ... pets that had filled the voids, provided affection and devotion. They loved her even if she wasn't deserving. How perfect that God had always given her creatures to feed and shelter and make secure, even though she hadn't always known comfort and security herself.

She and Henry were homeless themselves at the moment, but there was still the land and the dream. No animal would be turned away. None would be unloved. This would be a happy place.

Chapter 2

Lotsa Luck, Lady

W E'LL HAVE THAT house built in just a couple weekends," Uncle Ward said. "Before the snow flies."

"That soon?" Luanne asked into the phone, her voice rising with excitement. Her uncle from Springfield was their go-to expert in constructing log homes. He'd built one himself and said it went together in a snap. "That's great! We're bunking with Henry's son, but it's an hour commute every morning to get Randy in to school and me to work."

"Don't you worry. I'll be there to help."

"Okay! We'll let you know just as soon as the logs are delivered." She hung up, feeling hopeful. They were on the right path. They'd even come up with new, temporary living quarters. One of Henry's relatives connected him with another relative, who offered them his old camper. For free. With money so tight, they accepted without setting sight on the accommodations.

"You can just come get it and drive it right up to your place," the relative said.

Sounded perfect.

So that weekend they set out to pick up their new home, driving out in the country some two-and-a-half hours away. When they arrived, a skinny man with a cotton bucket hat and a full beard was standing by a dilapidated aqua blue school bus. "So where's the camper?" Luanne asked.

"Yer lookin' at it." The man proudly rocked back on his heels.

"This?" Luanne squinted.

"Yep. Converted her myself. She's a dream."

They pushed open the door—easier said than done, since there was no handle on the outside and just a long metal lever inside. The door folded open and the three climbed the treaded steps. Just in front of them was the driver's seat with its thick, red vinyl cushion with a gaping rip, facing an oversized steering wheel. The vehicle's owner paused. "See, take her wherever you want to go!"

A narrow rubber runner covered the aisle that was now considered a hallway. The front right corner of the converted camper contained a tiny gas stove, mini fridge, and a little sink. "Do they work?" Henry asked.

"Most of the time."

On the left side of the aisle one of the original bench bus seats was placed against the wall to form a couch. "Living room," the bearded man pointed out. Behind the kitchen, two bench seats had been positioned to face each other, with a table in between. "Dining room." A camping lantern sat on the table.

"Henry! No electricity!" Luanne whispered.

"Plenty of windows," Henry countered.

A bare, dusty double mattress on old wire box springs took up the back of the bus. "Bedroom!" the tour guide concluded. A makeshift divider separated the sleeping quarters from the living area. As a bonus,

13

there was even a closet-sized bathroom with a camping john, tiny shower, and sink.

They stepped back outside and Henry accepted the keys. "Does it run?" he asked.

"She oughta."

They shook hands and sealed the deal.

Luanne climbed into the station wagon to follow Henry as he drove the school bus/ camper back to their property. A big cloud of smoke kicked up as the makeshift mobile home shuddered to life. Its former owner waved goodbye, jumping up and down. Luanne realized later, that should have been a sign.

Unsure of the typical top speed for big aqua school buses, she figured this one was lucky to register thirty miles per hour going downhill in a stiff wind. With the hundred-mile trip back up into the mountains, they'd be running slower than sap. The bus lurched forward. They'd barely crawled out of sight of the driveway, however, when it sputtered to a stop. Henry turned the key, pushed the pedals and popped the hood, but couldn't get it started again. "I'll go back and get help," Luanne said. The previously jubilant relative hung his head at the prospect of the vehicle's return, but promised to tow the old bus back, fix it up, and have it right as rain by the next weekend.

Riding back home in the station wagon, Luanne let out a slow breath, accepting yet another roadblock to the dream. She gazed out the window at rows of small houses and farms and a goat standing beside a fence, chewing a mouthful of straw. A ray of September sun washed over the animal's swayed back. She smiled. She barely remembered her real mother or had a notion of any siblings. As an adult she'd been told of a half-sister, but until then she'd believed that she was an only child. But she remembered the goat.

LOVE

Luanne played in the prickly grass outside their home. She was old enough to keep herself busy for short periods of time, although still too little to stay up for long without Mama telling her that she needed a nap. Mama sat nearby, preparing some sort of vegetable over a bowl. Maybe she was shelling peas. Around the corner of the house peeked an animal—an ordinary brown goat. She was bigger than a dog, but not so large that Luanne felt afraid. Instead, she was filled with wonderful happiness.

A green collar circled the nanny's neck, with a copper bell that had lost its clapper. Broad, curved ears stuck out sideways like two wooden spoons, flopping over at the ends. The goat had beady little yellow eyes, each with a horizontal slit instead of a round dot in the middle. She wore a bemused expression, like she was laughing. Even her little pink mouth curved up in a smile. Her stubby tail flicked and, best of all, a scraggly beard hung from her chin—long, soft blonde hair that ended in a feathery point.

Although Mama seemed disinterested, Luanne picked a handful of long grass and offered it to her friend, who munched away with an odd sideways motion. Grass stuck out from puckered lips and gradually disappeared as the chomping progressed.

As far as she was concerned, Goat was a member of the family, although she lived out back by the woodshed and no one else seemed to like her. One time she saw Goat on the roof of the shed. Luanne thought Goat looked adorable way up there, but her father shouted, loud and angry, and threw rocks to shoo the goat down.

Another time Goat trotted over to greet her as she and Mama came out the door. Mama stepped aside, but Luanne threw herself against Goat's sturdy back. Goat let out a friendly bleat that made Luanne laugh with delight. She pressed her cheek against the animal's side. It felt warm from the sun. The warmth spread from her cheek until it blanketed her whole body. Without a doubt, she knew, that feeling was love.

Luanne didn't remember much about her childhood, but as an adult she had made contact with her half-sister Rose. Rose told her that she remembered the day their parents brought Luanne home from the hospital, swaddling her in soft cloth and laying her in a shoebox. "You were so tiny," Rose said, "You could fit in the palm of Daddy's hand." Her birth, by any account, was a medical miracle. She weighed only one pound. While it's uncommon but not unheard of for a mother today to successfully deliver such a tiny baby, in 1936 sophisticated neonatal intensive care units didn't exist. Medical science lacked our modern understanding of how to prevent potential infant heart and intestinal problems, treat underdeveloped respiratory systems, and boost immature immune systems. Most premature babies simply weren't expected to live.

When Luanne was born, a reporter was sent to the hospital to record the event. Luanne still kept the accompanying black and white photograph, yellowed with age, showing her stretched out next to a wooden ruler. She measured less than twelve inches long.

Rose told Luanne that the shoebox cradle was placed next to a source of heat—a lamp or the open oven door. It was the best incubator they could manage. Rose had told her everything she could about her mother. Then Luanne asked about the goat.

"Oh yes," Rose laughed. "When you were little you couldn't digest cow's milk. So the doctor suggested we get a goat."

"Did she have a name?"

"Not that I recall," Rose laughed. "I couldn't get near her. No one could. But when that goat saw you, she came running! She hated everyone else. Especially Daddy. He'd wrestle her onto the milking table, and she'd thrash to get away. One time when I watched him milk, she kicked him right in the forehead. So much blood. I remember it trickled into the pail and turned the milk pink. Did he ever swear then!"

"Was she really that bad? Because, I mean, I remember the goat. I really do. This may sound silly, but I thought she was my friend."

"I don't know if she was bad or not," Rose answered. "But Daddy hated her. He said he wished we'd never gotten that goat. Funny, because the goat, and her milk, were what helped keep you alive."

The rest of their mother's story did not have a happy ending. When Rose was eleven and Luanne was three, their mother was expecting another baby. While she was at the market one day, someone wheeled a heavy grocery cart abruptly around the end of an aisle. It slammed into the pregnant woman's stomach. Her cause of death was internal hemorrhaging. In the operating room, a baby boy was delivered but did not survive.

After that, Rose went away to live with relatives on her real father's side and lost contact with Luanne. Luanne thought it was sad that she never got to grow up with Rose. Sad that a mother could lose a baby like that in a grocery store. Luanne's heart ached for the baby boy who never had a chance. And her heart ached for her younger self, the little girl who was left all alone.

The funny little goat by the side of the road, however, evoked memories of her childhood nanny goat friend and made those hurts fade a little bit. Better to look ahead. She and Henry would soon be starting work on their very own log home and would return the next weekend to pick up their new living quarters.

When that day arrived, however, the bus made it just out of the town limits before choking to a halt. Steam billowed from under the hood.

"Maybe she just needs to cool down," Henry said. "Let's go get some lunch and come back." They drove off in the station wagon. When they returned, the bus was nowhere to be found.

"Are you sure this is the right road?" Luanne asked. "Did we miss a turn?"

"Look, here are the tire tracks. The bus was right here." Henry peered into the woods on the side of the road, as if maybe it had just wandered off.

"A bus doesn't simply go missing."

Another weekend passed before they could retrieve the bus from the garage where the vehicle, assumed abandoned, had been towed. This time Randy and Corky joined them. Luanne drove, following the bus, until it lurched to a stop on the shoulder of the highway. Henry got out and tinkered under the hood as cars sped by. Luanne walked the dog, who barked at the passing cars. Randy complained loudly out the car window. Henry had some words to say back. Then a siren wailed and a policeman joined the scene. He spoke to Henry and then brought Luanne to the cruiser. Corky barked frantically as Randy took his leash and pulled him back to the station wagon.

"Where are you coming from?" the officer asked, scribbling in his notebook.

"Over by Windsor, sir."

"And is that your bus?"

"Yes sir, I'd say so."

"Where are you headed?"

"Up Jeffersonville way."

"Why are you taking that bus?"

"We're going to live in it."

The officer took a second look at the rundown junker. "Why?"

"Because our tent blew away. Sir."

He stopped writing and cocked his head, looking at her, and then out at the beat-up bus and Henry half-swallowed under the hood, Randy hunkered down in the station wagon wiping sweat from his brow, and Corky sticking his head out the window, barking at each passing car. The officer heaved a sigh and shook his head. "Lotsa luck, Lady," he said, and snapped closed his notebook.

The school bus eventually made it all the way, barreling up the hill with no driveway at a reckless thirty miles per hour until it came to rest on a level grade beside the woods. Once she got out and saw it parked there, reality hit.

We can't live in a school bus. And then, *How can I ask Randy to live in a school bus?* She pushed the folding door open and climbed up the steps. What would he think of sleeping on a makeshift couch? She sat down on the hard vinyl seat. There was no privacy. No electricity. They had to fetch water from the brook down the road. He should go live with his father. He'd be better off. He'd have what a teenage boy needed.

But she wouldn't do it. She wouldn't even suggest it. She'd never make him feel unwanted as she had been as a child, passed around between relatives and sent away to live. If he wanted to stay, he'd have a home with them.

Randy enjoyed the novelty at first, but she could tell it wore on him. When he met a kid up the road who was in his same class at school, he spent more time hanging out there. Corky, however, took to the school bus right away. It was a step up from the tent. He didn't seem to mind where he slept, as long as Luanne stayed nearby. He did become anxious late at night, however, when the noises started. Little scratches in the walls. Rustling under the seats and behind the steering wheel. Corky whined and tried to poke his nose in the tight corners to find the culprits, but a squeak or squeal sent him running for the big bed in the back, where he pushed his head under a pillow.

"We need a cat," Luanne said.

Within days she heard about someone moving into an apartment who needed to find a new home for his cat. Beautiful, pure white Vicky looked too dainty for life in the country and too dignified to live in a second-rate camper. But there'd be plenty of mice to hunt.

At night the scratching and squeaking began. Luanne folded back the covers and slid into the big bed in the back. Help had arrived! "Vicky, you're on duty." She and Henry felt smugly confident that their troubles were over as they waited for action. The scratching grew louder, amplified by the thin metal walls. Corky sniffed reluctantly until a shrill chorus of squeaks sent him whimpering and bolting back to the bed. Before he could reach his destination, however, a blur of white passed him. He screeched to a stop and cocked his head at the quivering puff of fur that zoomed by and scooted under the pillow.

In one swift leap, Vicky had beaten him to the bed.

The first load of timber arrived at the end of September. A huge flatbed truck lumbered up the steep hill before sunup and unloaded the long logs. Henry built a bonfire to keep the workers warm.

Perhaps as optimistic as the dream of starting a farm and living off the land was the plan to build their own log home. Uncle Ward had ensured them they could do it and he'd help, but when he saw the piles of uncut logs, he clasped his hands to his weathered face in dismay. "Oh no! My log kit was all cut and numbered. It was like hammering together a big log puzzle. You're going to have to measure these logs, cut them, figure out where they all go...this isn't going to be a quick job at all."

Now he told them! Late fall, and the only work done was by a contractor who had installed an 850-foot gravel driveway up the hill and laid the foundation for the house. Now, in addition to all that cutting and measuring Uncle Ward described, they'd have to heft the logs, hammer the spikes, frame the windows and doors, wire the electricity—everything was left to their own devices. Henry was handy with tools and had helped in construction some, but Luanne couldn't tell a hammer from a screwdriver. As for opportunity, they both worked full-time weekdays. She was a teacher's aide and Henry made a simple but honest living cleaning carpets in people's homes. When would they have time to build a house? Perhaps the most concerning factor, she had to admit, was that they were no longer young. Not in the best of shape, either. A bit overweight. Henry had undergone surgery to treat ulcerated colitis caused by poor nutrition in the service in Guam. He'd had a heart attack in his forties. Forget about building a house, sometimes she worried that her husband might not live to see another day.

Are we crazy? Luanne wondered. Yet, she had no choice but to hope that somehow, some way or another, everything would work out. There was a plan greater than hers, she believed (she hoped), and although she wasn't sure what was in store, she wanted to trust in it. She just prayed that she would have the strength to get through whatever came her way.

Early one Saturday morning that October, Luanne stumbled out of the school bus, Corky at her heels. Noticing a light drizzle, she carried jackets for Henry and Randy, already at work. Randy tossed his long bangs out of his eyes and swung a hammer handily down on the boards framing the poured foundation. They had to cap over the basement before they could start laying logs, and they had to get it done soon before the winter weather took away the opportunity. The night before, they'd worked so late they had to light lanterns to continue. At the end of the day they'd boiled water in a big pot over the campfire and Henry had surprised them by cooking a lobster for dinner! Then Randy went inside and fell asleep on the couch that used to be a bus seat. Luanne realized that he'd never once complained.

Corky lifted his paws dramatically above the tall grass. "No, I don't have a raincoat for you," Luanne said. The dog hated getting wet. "Go back inside where it's dry," she pointed to the bus. But Corky wanted to be with her and trotted along in the dampness, whining as he walked. One time he'd cut his paw, a surface wound really, yet he'd cried and rolled his eyes and pouted worse than a toddler who'd dropped his lollipop. Days later, when Luanne tenderly cradled his foot in her hand to make sure the cut was healing, he'd rolled onto his back, waved his other three legs in the air, and let out a sound so mournful, it nearly made Luanne cry as well. Weeks after the cut was completely healed, Corky still made a show of hobbling, holding up his paw, and whimpering for attention.

He could cry and sulk, and no doubt he could also smile. Whenever he saw Luanne, he ran up to her with a huge grin on his face. If she was away for the whole day, he'd bound up and greet her, wagging his tail furiously and smiling, he was just so happy to be with her again. He responded the same way, too, if she'd only left the room for a few minutes. Whenever he saw her, it was as if she'd been missing for weeks. Maybe he wasn't the most brilliant dog, but his heart held an endless capacity to love.

Luanne patted the dog's head and then pushed her hands into her sweatshirt pockets. In a matter of weeks the first frost would cover the ground. Geese overhead honked noisily, heading south for the winter. Everything pointed to the approaching cold weather, but they were nowhere near ready.

"Sill's done, and half the floor joists," Henry greeted, straddling the foundation wall. The house was cut into the side of a hill so that the poured cement wall was tall enough for a door and windows in the front, and the back was mostly underground. It didn't look like much now, but when it was finished the house would feature a full walk-in basement, an open first floor with a porch, and a sleeping loft.

Corky followed Luanne, straying only to wander under a balcony of nearby evergreens, the needles dripping liquid on his curly head. He shook and whimpered again. "Weather's not helping any." Luanne handed the men their jackets. "I needed three blankets last night." They wouldn't be able to live in an unheated school bus much longer. She knelt and helped Henry lift a new board into position. "If it doesn't stop raining and we don't get this covered over, our basement's going to become another pond!"

When the construction workers dug the foundation, she'd asked if they might just scoop out a small pond at the base of the hill. Just big enough for a few ducks. She even pictured a lovely pair of swans there. It seemed as if she'd just turned her back, and when she looked again her charming little pond was actually a gaping fourteen feet deep and fifty feet across.

"How do we get this thing filled up?" Luanne had asked, wondering what in heaven's name she'd just done. There wasn't extra money to have water pumped in. No one wanted an unsightly pit on their beautiful land. "What if we're stuck with a hole in our yard forever?"

But everyone assured her that underground springs and water coming down off the mountains would do the trick. The next day it had started raining, and it rained every day for nearly a week. The pond was filled.

If only a house could be constructed just as quickly. They would have to finish capping over the basement before they could install their first row of logs. She and Henry still had to go to work, and it had been the wettest fall she could remember. Winter would be setting in soon. What if they couldn't do it? What if they really didn't know what they were doing?

"Mom, check it out. Look at Corky!" Randy called, pausing his hammer for a moment.

She looked down to the pond. Corky had ventured away and stood near the edge, up to his chest in water. He looked back toward her woefully, as if to say "What am I doing here?"

Is he stuck in the mud? she wondered. Why had he gone in, anyway? He hated getting wet. It didn't make any sense, but there he was. She called to him loudly and his ears perked. He turned, as if this turning around idea hadn't crossed his mind, and slogged his way out of the mud, shaking his paws when he got to the bank.

Maybe what they were doing didn't make any sense either. But it felt right. It just felt right.

Chapter 3

Three Little Gray Chickens

LUANNE WALKED ALONG the side of the road, a heavy plastic bucket slapping against her knee. There was a well on their property, but it was often dry, so they collected crystal clear, mountain-fed water from a nearby stream. Usually Henry brought the tractor down and filled a 50-gallon drum. But this day he was out and she needed water, so she gathered just one bucketful. Likely this was her last chance to draw from the stream before it froze.

Corky pranced a bit ahead, disappearing at times to explore the gulley, but always checking back to make sure Luanne was right behind. She could see his curly fur dotted with prickly burdocks she'd need to pick off later. A car approached and she stepped to the side of the road, the bucket jostling, dripping frigid water down her leg. It was Henry. He stopped so that she and Corky could climb in. His face flushed with guilt.

A cacophony of cackles erupted from the back as Luanne balanced the bucket on the floorboards. She looked at Henry and smiled. "What did you do now?"

He was supposed to have gone to town for a dozen eggs. What he got instead was a six-pack of beer, eight white Leghorn chickens, and eight Rhode Island Reds. They clucked loudly from crates in the back.

"We'll never have to buy eggs again!" he beamed.

That afternoon Henry and Randy hammered together a lopsided coop from leftover scraps of wood. The chickens squawked in their boxes, unhappy at being pent up, waiting. Most people would have built the coop first and then bought the chickens.

And, with so much work still to be done on the house, Luanne was angry at first. But chickens! She reached through the slats of the wooden crates to stroke the soft feathers. Their very own chickens!

By dusk Henry had gone through a box of nails and three bandages, but produced a serviceable henhouse. Luanne picked up the empty beer cans on the ground. *All six?* But Henry had been working hard and she quickly pushed the worry away.

"Don't we need a pen too?" she asked.

"Free range," Henry responded. He opened the crates and chickens scattered everywhere, clucking and causing a horrible racket. They fluttered their wings, ran on their scrawny feet, and pecked at the ground. Corky's ineffective herding only caused them to spread out farther. As it grew dark, instinctively the chickens headed for the coop and settled onto the roosts. Henry closed the door to keep them safe for the night.

The next day as Luanne did her chores, the chickens pecked away underfoot. She smiled. They paraded around with cheerful, bossy clucks and bobbing heads. When she tried to pick them up, most scurried away, except for Penny. Penny was the smallest chicken, with stubby auburn feathers and short little legs. After Luanne scattered the corn, Penny always scuttled up and pecked Luanne's ankle. Luanne concluded that was her way of saying thank-you. She bent down and stroked Penny's back, and sometimes lifted her, crossing her arms over the warm, feathery body. Most chickens didn't like to be held but then again, if you had enough chickens, you'd find one who was different.

Luanne discovered something else about chickens. One night just as it grew dark, she started to close up the henhouse and did a double-take. There were the eight white chickens lined up on the roost on one side of the coop. The eight red chickens roosted on the other side. Not one chicken mixed with those of a different color.

"Why do they do that?" she asked Henry.

"Danged if I know."

"How do they know what color they are?"

Every night the chickens segregated themselves in the henhouse. Luanne assumed, as she did about dogs and other animals, that chickens were colorblind. But some instinct must have told them which birds belonged together. Something deeply ingrained that warned them it was not okay to intermingle.

Later than usual one night, Luanne and Henry rushed to close up the henhouse. Hearing a ruckus, she peered into the dark coop and counted the chickens to make sure they were all there. Eight red ones on one side. Eight white ones on the other. And three gray ones in the middle.

Startled, she stepped back. Of course, they didn't have any gray chickens. She squinted and looked again. There on the rod sat three baby raccoons, hanging on for dear life. Their wide eyes shone in the dark. Caught in the act!

"Shoo!" she gasped, scanning the roosts again to make sure all the chickens were accounted for. The raccoons scooted down from the perch and skedaddled out of the coop.

"Go on home now," Henry called.

She and Henry laughed at the retreating raccoons—more frightened than the chickens—and latched the henhouse door. The raccoons' little fat bodies wriggled as they ran. They laughed even harder when a loud, angry chattering rose from back in the woods.

"They're getting a scolding!" Henry hooted.

Luanne clutched her side. "Their mama's saying, 'We told you not to wander off so far. Why didn't you let us know where you were going!'"

"And the papa's scolding them, 'You didn't even bring home a chicken dinner!'"

The two returned to the bus, bent over laughing. The dressing-down from the woods subsided, and everyone went to bed safe and snug.

Luanne knew she'd have to be extra-careful securing the coop. She loved the chickens and vowed to keep them safe and happy. And, to that point, she began thinking it might be a great idea to get a rooster. Just as that thought crossed her mind, neighbors up the road decided that they no longer wanted their rooster and asked if she and Henry could take him off their hands.

Why someone would want to get rid of a rooster soon became clear.

Fred was a handsome fellow, and he knew it. The minute he was dropped off and let out of his box, he pulled himself up so that his legs looked remarkably long and he high-stepped around the yard. He must have thought he was in heaven upon spying the yard full of attractive females. He puffed his striking speckled chest and stuck his tiny pointy beak in the air. His body shone in rich brown and black as if polished, but most of all he loved to display his impressive tail feathers. So dark they were almost blue, with a speck of white, they curled gracefully and cascaded down behind. He puffed and strutted some more. The hens eyed him curiously, but when they approached, he dashed after them with a gleam in his eye and frightened them away.

This perplexed Fred. Every day the same thing. The more he pursued the ladies, the more they ran off. Luanne felt sorry for him even though he crowed too early in the morning and tried to dash after her, too, when she approached with food.

"How am I going to teach Fred some manners?" she asked, scattering the seed.

"He might make a nice stew," Henry suggested.

Luanne tried to catch Fred so that she could hold him and introduce him to Penny. But Fred would have none of it. He was the boss around there, and he'd decide who and when he wanted to visit.

"He's not for you, Penny," Luanne sighed. "There will be other roosters in the barnyard." Actually, after experiencing life with Fred she hoped not, but Luanne didn't want her beautiful red-feathered friend to feel bad about Fred's poor manners. Penny ran off and joined the others.

Luanne needn't have worried, however, because barnyard karma prevailed. The hens knew that they had Fred outnumbered. Every time Fred started to pursue one of the lovely ladies, the other chickens raced over from near and far. Squawking and clucking, they surrounded the rooster and began pecking. He'd pounce on a red chicken by the woodpile, and soon be set upon by her fuming friends. He'd trail a couple of white hens around the side yard and find himself amid a horde of heated hens.

One afternoon Luanne and Henry heard a huge commotion of crowing and clucking, and ran out to the coop. The girls were angry and feathers were flying. Luanne caught a glimpse of Fred bobbing and weaving, the hens blocking his escape. He looked so defeated that her heart ached for him. It wasn't always the little ones who got picked on. He might have been a big bully at first, but now he was being assaulted. They'd nearly pecked him bald-headed. His once-beautiful tail hung with just a few tattered, dirty feathers. She couldn't bear to watch. She grabbed a broom to intervene. "Mean or not, he doesn't deserve this."

Henry held her back. "He'll be alright," he said. "That is, if he shapes up."

"There won't be anything left of him to shape up."

Henry chuckled. "You wait and see. If he wants to live with the ladies, he'll have to change his ways fast."

The next day, Luanne and Henry began the final steps of capping off the basement. As usual, the weather wasn't cooperating and a strong wind had kicked up. Luanne sat on the end of the roll of tar paper to keep it from blowing away. She slopped down a glob of tar with a wide spatula. The wind blew the black gook back across her shirt. Another blob slapped her in the face. As she wiped the mess from her cheek, the hens' hullabaloo started up again.

She jumped off the roof and rushed toward the scene. This time she'd help poor Fred. He shouldn't have to endure such abuse.

As she rounded the corner and saw the scene, however, she stopped short. Fred stood a respectful distance from the hens. He found a grain of cracked corn in the dirt and began scratching. "Brock, brock," he called to the hens, and then stepped back. The chickens converged, gobbled the corn and waited for more. Fred led them around the yard, locating corn, and then standing back to let them eat their fill.

"Would you look at this!" she called to Henry. Fred had become a gentleman and earned the respect of the ladies.

Snow topped the distant mountains first and then sprinkled down to the hillsides and valleys. Corky chased a few scattered flakes and then returned to Luanne. She pulled off her woolen gloves and spread fresh hay in the chicken coop. They'd need to make some improvements to keep the flock snug and warm for the winter. Not to mention doing something about their own living space. She shifted her gaze to the school bus. The November air felt just as frigid inside their home as out. Time left for comfortable living in the modest, unheated, pseudo-camper was fleeting, if not already past.

They had limited options for alternate living places. They could maybe stay with friends or one of the kids for a while, but the kids lived scattered about, some out of state, and she didn't want to impose. With the dog, cat, chickens, and rooster, they couldn't very well pick up and leave. Besides, she didn't want to leave. This was home.

What was there to do? She walked a few yards over to the unfinished house and ran her hand along one of the logs. They'd spent every available moment working, with scarves wrapped around their necks, feeling the pressure of the changing seasons. Pressure that weighed her down like a heavy wool coat.

Corky barked and Luanne looked up to see what had captured his attention. She edged down the little hill into which the foundation was dug. Even though only a few rows of logs framed the top of the home, the basement was complete. Solid floor joists and plank decking capped over the cellar hole. Corky stood at the door. She peered in the window. While the walls and floor were made of cold, uninviting cement, the basement offered shelter. By some stretch of the imagination, you might even call it cozy. It wasn't conventional. It wasn't ideal. But her family would be protected from the elements this winter. She closed her eyes, trying to envision the dream. It was still far away.

Although their new home was quite literally a hole in the ground, Luanne considered it one step closer to living in her dream home.

From the outside, the front of the poured cement basement stood about eight foot high in the middle, just tall enough for a white metal exterior door with nine small panes of glass. Two sets of larger casement windows decked out the front, on either side of the door. Above this, eventually, would span a porch accessed from the main floor living room. The land sloped, so that you had to manage an incline to get to the left corner of the house. The other two sides and the back sat mainly underground, with only small utility windows.

Despite the door and windows in the front, the interior was dark and cold. Luanne and Henry had retrieved what few furnishings—beds, mainly—they'd managed to store at a friend's unused summer camp, and spread an old braided rug over the cement floor.

Just as they were becoming known as people who'd never refuse a homeless or unwanted animal, word also got out that they'd take in stray furnishings. Someone they met at the general store gave them an old refrigerator. Uncle Ward brought over an old jelly cupboard. A neighbor down the road had a barn full of leftover plumbing and supplies, and set them up with bathroom facilities, all for free. A secondhand wood-burning stove soon provided welcome warmth.

"All this space!" Luanne said. She finished hanging a curtain around the improvised bathroom. "We even have a powder room."

"Looks more like an outhouse," Randy said.

"You'll be glad it's inside once the snow falls." Luanne hummed as she arranged folding lawn chairs in the living room area.

Henry laughed. "Look at you, you'd almost think you're enjoying this."

"I am," she said. "Besides, this is fun. I feel like a pioneer woman setting up her soddy. I'm sure we have it better than what they had to contend with. Real windows. A real door. I'm just excited to actually be in the house!"

"Not much of a house yet. But ... here's a table for you." Henry hoisted a wooden plank between two sawhorses, stood back, looked at it, and frowned. "Wait a minute." He took off outside. When he returned, he held something hidden behind his back. He located an empty iced tea jar, filled it with water from the bucket and then slowly revealed a fistful of fading

Black-eyed Susans and a few stray weeds that had survived the autumn frost. Plopping them in the jar and setting it on the table, he said, "Better."

"Best!" Luanne said, embracing him. "Now it's a home for real."

They had the woodstove for heating and a real range that ran on propane gas and a microwave for cooking. A jug for water that (now that the stream was beginning to freeze over) they filled up in town. A flush toilet, sink and bathtub. A coop of contented chickens and a rooster outside. And a cat and a dog to curl up at their feet. That evening, after climbing into her old metal-framed bed while a cozy fire crackled, Luanne drifted into a happy and peaceful sleep, content that her little family was together and imagining how many more animals could join them there.

A few days later Luanne and Henry returned from some errands, lugging bags of groceries into the basement. Corky usually greeted them at the door, waiting there with his goofy grin, but he was nowhere to be found. Luanne walked around by the chicken coop, then up near the edge of the woods, and then all the way down the driveway, calling his name.

"Was he here when you came home from school?" she asked Randy.

"I didn't see him," he answered.

She busied herself in the kitchen area, anxiously staring out the front door window, expecting to hear the jingle of the tags on his collar at any moment. When it grew dark and there was still no sign of him, she sank down in one of the webbed chairs and buried her head in her hands.

"He's just exploring," Henry said, rubbing her shoulder. But Luanne knew better. Corky'd never left the property before. Had he been lonely and run off to find her? Had something frightened him away? Was he hurt?

Henry and Randy drove up and down the dirt road, scanning the ditches along the side. Luanne was partly relieved when they didn't find him—that meant he hadn't been hit by a car, she hoped. She squeezed her eyes tight. *Please, God, don't let him be hurt. Or worse...* She tried not to think about it, but panic closed in around her chest. How could she ever go on without her Corky?

COMFORT

When Luanne was a young girl, she knew a thing or two about instability. Her real mother died when she was three. Her second mother died when she was seven, and her father and her third mother divorced. She'd lived with relatives and strangers. But a dog—now that was one thing that remained constant. Or at least, in the beginning, the desire for one.

There'd been no dog in her first home. Luanne had only scattered memories of her first mama, and her second mother had mostly stayed alone in a dark room, sick with tuberculosis. All Luanne knew was she'd had to tiptoe around the house and be quiet. A noisy dog, or even a frisky cat, would have been foolish in that situation. But when she was seven years old, her father married young and pretty Millie. It didn't look to Luanne like Millie was preparing to die anytime soon. With such fortuitous timing, Luanne hoped that maybe she could at last have a dog. She'd begged her daddy for so long. And then, one fall day, it happened.

Luanne had been sitting on a kitchen chair, whispering to her doll with the china head and watching Millie pace the linoleum and stare at the clock. They'd lived in a town located in the heart of Vermont's machine tool industry, and nearly half the town's residents worked at the gear-shaping factory. That morning her dad had run out on a quick errand, and she could tell Millie would likely give him a combing out if they were late for work.

Millie paused from her pacing and scowled at Luanne. "Put that raggedy doll down and get moving," she said, eyes narrowing. "Only an imbecile talks to her doll."

Luanne flushed, ashamed. The doll wasn't beautiful to most people, she knew. Dingy dress, a crack across her cheek, bald patches on her scalp. But Luanne thought she looked like an angel. They'd always been together. She hugged the doll tightly to her chest.

Before long Daddy's boots clomped up the steps and he swung through the screen door, hefting a bushel basket.

"What on earth?" Millie looked angry enough to bite a nail in two.

"I got it, just like I told you I would!" Daddy said, smiling broadly. By the way the basket jiggled, Luanne knew something alive was inside.

"What is it?" she gushed. "Can I see?"

Millie glared into the basket, her face contorting. "I *told* you *not* to." She poked a manicured finger inside the slatted container. "What kind of hunting you plan on doing with that?"

"He'll grow," Bill returned, straightening his shoulders. "Make a fine rabbit hound."

"Can I see?" Luanne repeated, rising to her tiptoes. "Oh!" A shivering beagle pup huddled against the side of the basket. Her voice fell to a murmur. "Ohhhhhhh." She stroked his neck, and his tiny pink tongue attacked her hand. She let his sharp little teeth nibble on her thumb. "Is he really ours? Can I hold him?" It was almost too good to be true. She lifted the pup out of the basket. He squirmed so she set him gently on the floor where he wobbled around, nose to the ground, snuffling dust in the corners.

Her father let loose an easy, boyish laugh. "See, he's on the trail of something already." All at once the dog stopped. His neck stretched, his tummy tucked, and his body heaved. He gasped out a glob of slimy goo.

"Eww." Millie snatched a rag off the counter. "I won't have that disgusting hound dirtying up my floors. Do you hear me?"

Her father shook his head and scooped up the dog. "C'mon, back in the basket, Upchuck." And so the dog was named.

Later, Luanne told Grammie Worth, Millie's mom who lived next door, about the dog. "Daddy says Upchuck has to stay in the basket."

"Upchuck?" Her grandma twisted her face into a scowl.

"Our new puppy. We just got him."

"What kind of a name is that for a dog?"

Luanne shrugged. "I don't know. What's it mean?"

"Never mind. It's not ladylike. Now go fetch me my cup of tea."

Every day Luanne hurried home from school and raced to the backyard to play with Upchuck. Her father built the dog a small pen. It broke her heart to see the puppy locked away. He should be free to run and explore his new home without a scolding. Her fingers rushed to unlock the latch and swing open the gate. At least she would play with him every afternoon. The beagle jumped up and kissed her, and then raced around the yard, tail rotating in helicopter circles. He never strayed for long without returning to check in with Luanne, push his wet nose against her cheek and nudge her side with his paw. She laughed at his playfulness. After a while he'd tire and she'd run inside to get her doll. The three of them would sit together in the grass under the maple tree all afternoon.

"I'm an imbuckle," she said, not quite understanding the word. "I'm not supposed to talk to you or to my doll, either." She picked up the dog and pressed him against her. A sweet warmth swelled in her heart. "But I will," she whispered.

From inside the house, the sounds of her father and Millie arguing wafted out the open windows. "They don't want me," she confided to her two special friends beside her. "They don't care. But you do." She looked into the pup's soft eyes. The dog kissed her neck. He kissed the doll's cracked china head too. Maybe this was what it felt like to be a family. Maybe this was what it felt like to be loved.

Chapter 4

Slide On In

EVERY MORNING FOR days—for weeks—Luanne tromped in the snow, searching the woods behind the house and the pasture below, calling Corky's name. She put up a sign at the general store and asked everyone in town. Every afternoon she drove slowly home from work, taking different side roads, peering up driveways. Before bed every night, she fell to her knees. "God, please protect your sweet creature, Corky. Keep him safe." And then, not truly trusting it was possible, "and please, bring him home to us."

Then one night she could pray no longer. Her faithful friend was gone. The bright moon shone through the window. Henry put a log in the fire. Randy fixed a snack. And Luanne let the tears fall.

When she dusted off her knees and climbed into bed, she had only enough energy to lie there, staring at the beams across the ceiling. The night was strangely quiet, amplifying her dismal thoughts. She was not worthy of a dog as special as Corky. If only she'd shown him just how much she loved him, just how important he was to her, maybe he wouldn't have left. If only ... a movement at the door caught her attention. A face in the window. A face with thick tan curls and a little gray on top. Brown fur mixed with black and white. Coloring from every breed seen 'round the country back roads. The homeliest dog she'd ever seen.

"Corky!!"

Everyone jumped up and ran for the door at the same time, but she got there first. She threw open the door and Corky limped into her arms and kissed her. "Good dog," she said over and over. Everyone crouched down and patted him, and Randy got him some water.

"Where have you been?" she cried. His fur was dirty and matted. His eyes drooped and even his ears hung limply. He whined softly, but when he looked up at her, he smiled.

That night she held him, cradling his head, stroking his neck as he dozed. He slept the entire next day, too tired even to eat. She applied ointment to his cut paws. In a few days, he was back to his old self again.

"Don't ever leave me again." She kissed the top of his head. "I'll be good," she whispered. He seemed to tell her the same thing.

Down the road and around the bend stood a crooked old sugarhouse in a field behind a peeling, blue clapboard farmhouse. The structure was just a rustic shack with a skinny chimney where someone used to boil sap to make maple syrup. Their route took them past the sugarhouse often, and they always noted it was loaded with wood. Outside too. Stacks of it. They could see the wood from the road. The shack hadn't produced maple syrup in years. The house beside it appeared abandoned too.

"Look at that wood," Randy sighed. "And lots of it." He pressed his forehead against the car window. "Doubt anyone still lives there. Probably nobody even remembers it's here."

The car slowed. "What a waste," Henry added.

That winter Henry hadn't been feeling well and his carpet cleaning business suffered. Money was tight and something always needed repair. They tried to prioritize expenditures. Food and health care for themselves, Randy and the animals made the top tier. Drilling a new well would have to wait. They had to buy the used Ford pickup with the snowplow so that they could pave a way up and down the long driveway. Heat was a necessity, but firewood that was cut, split and seasoned was a luxury. Three times that winter they'd run out of firewood. Although the back of the property was wooded, chopping down trees was hard work and if the tree was too tall, the job was dangerous. Many of the trees were pines, which weren't good for burning. Sometimes they picked up logs and branches on the ground, but often they were wet or rotten. So despite the abundance of trees, firewood remained a critical problem. One time they burned a rickety old chair. Luanne borrowed extra blankets to pile high on their beds and hung plastic to cover the windows. She encouraged Randy to sleep over at his friend's house when temperatures dipped. She even prepared snug dens away from the draft for Corky and Vicky. But the chill still cut right through the walls. Once, they'd thanked their lucky stars when they'd discovered the unbelievably low-priced Midnight Firewood Service. But when the delivery actually arrived at midnight, under the cover of darkness, they doubted the service's integrity. Now there was no extra money for firewood and Henry was sick. His cough shook his body until his muscles ached. Luanne bit her lip and glanced at the sugarhouse. She had to admit, she was tempted. "Maybe we could just borrow some. We could pay it back."

Henry stopped in the middle of the road to consider the situation.

"You're sick. I can't just watch you catch your death of pneumonia," she reasoned. "And Randy. And the animals are cold. Maybe we were meant to find this wood."

They looked at each other and then back at the sugarhouse. Then they both shook their heads. "No, we can't. It's not ours," Luanne sighed, and Henry pulled away.

Maybe they'd make it through the rest of the winter without a problem. March weather was unpredictable. It had already come in hard and, if the old adage held true, could turn out mild as a lamb in another week.

That next day, however, a howling winter storm bore down. Henry coughed violently, unable to get out of bed. Luanne put a hand to his red-hot forehead. "You've got to go to the hospital now." She bundled him up in a sweater and helped him into his coat. Freezing rain pelted the car as she drove to the emergency room. Her knuckles turned white as she gripped the wheel.

"It's pneumonia," the doctor said, asking a nurse to start the admission process. "We'll keep you here tonight to get those antibiotics working."

It was a mixed blessing. At least he'd be warm that night.

Luanne called Randy, who was at his friend's house down the road, and asked him if he'd be able to stay there overnight, but to check on the animals first.

"Okay," Randy said, "Hope you aren't trying to come home tonight. Roads are a mess."

The nurses let Luanne sleep in the reclining chair next to Henry's bed. Unfortunate that it took a hospital stay to be warm. Henry responded to the medication, and the discharge papers came through the next day, along with a handful of instructions and prescriptions. Luanne squeezed his hand. "We'll get you home."

The roads weren't much better that morning. In Vermont there are five seasons: summer, autumn, winter, spring, and mud—a time that is no longer winter and not yet spring. It starts with the slow drip of melting snowbanks and thawing frost turning the ground into spongy earth. Water trickles down from the mountaintops. Then the whole melted mess flows down the dirt roads, washing away the gravel, creating impassable ruts. While some people complained about the inconveniences of that time of year, Henry would just sigh and say, "Soon enough, mud season will pass. Of course, the mud will always come again."

Luanne drove slowly down the rutted roads, making a quick stop at the drugstore. She almost passed by the general store when she hit the brake and turned in. "I'll take a bundle of firewood," she told the cashier, "and could you have a cord delivered?" Another bill might not get paid, but she was buying the wood. Her family would not be so cold again.

The added weight of the wood in the back gave the car enough traction to make its way up the slippery driveway. Washed out gullies, branches carried down from the woods, and trails of ice scarred the yard. The cellar door hung partly open.

"Maybe Randy's come home to take care of the dog." Luanne said, helping Henry down the slope to the basement.

The ground was uneven and she always had to be careful when walking there, even in the best weather conditions. But with the freezing rain, a weak-with-pneumonia, two-hundred-pound man on one arm, and a bag of cough medicines and Kleenex balanced under the other, the task was even more difficult.

Then, things got worse.

When she pushed the door all the way open, she gasped and steadied herself against the sill. The weather had invited itself inside.

"Whoa," murmured Henry.

The basement was covered in muddy ice. The table legs appeared cemented to the floor and the water jug tipped, frozen mid-spill. Henry's work boots had floated across the room and remained upright, side by side, as if some phantom had taken a walk and then disappeared. Corky and Vicky huddled together on the big metal-framed bed, half-burrowed under the pillows. Corky wriggled and wagged, but didn't move from his nest to greet them.

Luanne's knees buckled. She wasn't sure she could hold up Henry, let alone herself. The doctor's instructions were to keep Henry warm and dry. No one had accounted for a mudslide in the house.

STRENGTH

The very name of the building indicated that this was a place for children who were parentless, but Luanne was not an orphan. The summer before her eighth birthday her father told her to pack a suitcase and drove her away from home. They rode out past the factories, past the little corner store that sold penny mint juleps, past rows of houses that were packed close together and then spread out farther and farther. Cows and red barns dotted the land, stretching to where there was nothing but green hills and trees and puffy clouds in the sky. Her father turned onto a dirt driveway that led to a large brick building with tall windows, flanked by two other brick buildings. A small wooden sign hanging above the front door read KURN HATTIN HOME FOR GIRLS.

Luanne got out and stood by the fender of the Buick, suitcase at her feet. It contained a few dresses, a hairbrush, and a coat and hat for the winter. She stared at her scuffed white tennis shoes.

"Are you picking me up tonight?" she asked.

"No."

"This weekend?"

"No," he said.

"What about Millie?"

"You know about Millie. You know we're getting a divorce."

Even though Millie had complained and told Luanne that she was in the way and called her hurtful names, Luanne didn't want Millie to leave. And more importantly, Luanne didn't want to leave her father. "I'm old enough to help. I'll do anything you want. I can cook. And mend. Please, Daddy. Why can't I stay?"

Bill nodded at a woman with a clipboard. He jingled the keys in his pocket as she approached.

"When are you coming back for me?" Luanne's thumb moved gently across her arm as if she were stroking Upchuck's soft ear.

The woman with the clipboard wore a plain blue dress with crisp pleats and tiny mother-of-pearl buttons up the front. She bent to greet Luanne, her loose gray hair falling in front of her face. Then, rising, she spoke to Bill for a moment. "I believe we're all set," the director said after a bit, and lifted Luanne's luggage.

"Daddy, don't go," Luanne barely whispered. "I'll be good."

The car door slammed, tires ground against the dirt road, and her father drove off.

As much as she missed home, she discovered that Kurn Hattin was not the dreary place of storybooks and fairy tales. The housemother sat and rubbed her shoulders when she cried. The teachers praised her skills when she sewed a straight seam. They were strict, also, and just as quickly ripped out a seam not perfectly done. Luanne didn't mind; as long as she knew the rules, she tried hard to be good. There was only one problem. No animals. Deer and raccoons lived in the woods. The field harbored sparrows and hermit thrush. Even ants and bees. But no pet for Luanne.

Kurn Hattin housed only girls. A corresponding home known as the Boys' Department was located over in Westminster, several miles away. Kurn Hattin's little school bus passed it by whenever the girls went into town to go to church. *I wish I was a boy,* Luanne silently prayed every time they neared. From the road, she could see the Boys' Department's barns, and behind the pasture fence—cows and a horse.

Luanne thought of that beautiful roan horse when she was playing, running in the lush field. Her short bob flopped in the wind. She wished she could grow it long, like a mane.

She thought of the horse, too, at night when it was dark, and she couldn't sleep because of the scary noises.

Luanne stayed in Warren House, which held two big dorm rooms with an archway between them. The younger kids slept in the first room. Luanne shared the larger dorm room with more than a dozen others. The girls slept in cots, eight along the wall on one side, eight along the other side.

Every night the housemother, Miss Willie, checked to make sure the girls had brushed their teeth. They quickly learned that Miss Willie checked only the toothbrushes but not their teeth, so they just ran their toothbrushes under the water. Luanne took her bath once a week in one of the big claw-foot tubs on either side of the bathroom. She usually rushed in and out of the tub, hiding herself behind a towel.

Although the teachers and staff were kind, they were also strict, and rules, such as bedtime promptly at eight o'clock, were to be obeyed. After eight, the only noise in the room came from Miss Willie's radio. The housemother's room was just beyond a thin wall, and unfortunately the older woman's hearing wasn't what it used to be.

When it was inky dark Luanne heard the strange noises. A spooky creak emanated from Miss Willie's room. Luanne peeked out from the covers. *Was that a chair in the corner? Or a ghost?*

Eerie organ tones slithered out from Miss Willie's radio. A deep, maniacal cackle. A voice as dark as Satan himself. "Who knows what evil lurks in the hearts of men?"

Luanne shrank under the covers.

"The Shadow knows! Bwa ha ha ha." Then came the sound of a squeaky door opening. "Welcome to the Inner Sanctum," a deep voice said. The radio static crackled. Dark, mysterious voices continued, but Luanne pulled her pillow over her head to block them out.

Why Miss Willie enjoyed such frightening radio shows, Luanne never knew. But every night she did her best to get to sleep quickly so she wouldn't hear the squeaky door or the evil Shadow. Sometimes, some of the girls talked and giggled after Lights Out. That was never good.

Miss Willie would stomp in from her room. "All right," she'd call, "Everyone at attention."

"Attention" was one of the consequences for misbehavior. All the girls had to get out of bed and stand in line for what felt like hours. Luanne's legs buckled as she tried to stand. All she wanted was to curl up back on her cot, but she couldn't because if she did, Miss Willie would be angry. Luanne's knees quivered, but when she closed her eyes, the beautiful horse at the Boys' Department came to her rescue. She could almost see it, loping along the fence line beside the road, muscles rippling. She imagined having strong muscles too. Strong muscles to get her through. When at last she lay back down to bed, she pulled the soft blanket up as high as it would go and felt as if the horse was nuzzling her cheek.

One day, Miss Willie announced, "We're going into town to the movies. We're going to see *The Secret Garden*."

Luanne felt her stomach twist. She'd had enough of Miss Willie's late night radio shows, and something about the mysterious movie title gave her the shivers. "Do I have to go?" she whispered.

"Don't you want to see the movie?"

Luanne shook her head.

"*The Secret Garden* is a beautiful movie."

"I don't think so," she sniffed.

The housemother laughed gently. "Oh, Luanne. Just go. You'll love it. I promise." She led her onto the bus with the others.

Luanne sat in the darkened theater. She hugged her arms around herself, unconvinced. Especially when the unhappy orphan Mary arrived at the vast, creepy manor in the equally dark and dreary English moorland.

But when Mary and her friend Dickon entered the garden, the movie magically transformed from black and white to brilliant, magnificent color. Little buds pushed out of the earth, grew, and bloomed. Luanne sat up in her seat. The color blossomed around her. Nothing else mattered anymore; she was captivated.

Although Mary was the lonely, parentless character with whom Luanne would logically find common ground, it was Dickon she felt drawn to. Dickon belonged to the moorland as if he'd sprouted there like the heather and the grass. Luanne couldn't stop staring at him. He spoke gently, with an inexplicable wisdom beyond his young years.

Luanne held her breath as Mary earnestly told Dickon about a garden she found. Mary wondered how to tell if the garden was dead.

"I'll know." Dickon said. Luanne nodded. Yes, he would know.

She felt drawn into his strength, his ability to comprehend the natural world around him. Wherever he walked, he was surrounded by his animal friends. Rabbits followed him. A fox ate from his hand. Birds perched on his shoulder. He even played a small wooden pipe that he used to charm the creatures. "The animals tell me all their secrets," Dickon said in the movie. "Sometimes I think perhaps I'm a bird, or a fox, or a squirrel ... and I don't know it."

That was how Luanne felt too! Or at least, how she wished she could feel. Not only to be a part of the animals she loved, but as if she were one of them! What a gift. Luanne watched the rest of the movie with hardly a breath, as Mary and Dickon helped heal a crippled boy, saved a garden, and brought a broken family together. Near the end, Dickon rode off into the lifting fog on his moor pony. Luanne felt the hooves pound on the grass, the thick mane rustle in the breeze, the muscles flex and reach. The pony was beautiful, strong and free, and Luanne was the moor pony.

Luanne needed the strength of a team of moor horses to help her contend with the frozen muck all over the log home's basement floor, and Henry sick with pneumonia.

"I'd better help clean this up," Henry said between coughs.

"Oh no, you don't! I promised the doctor I'd keep you warm, and that's what I'm going to do."

She wanted to take charge and handle everything, but a little tiny voice inside her nipped away, telling her that she really wasn't capable of doing this. Maybe it was true. For the millionth time, she wondered what they'd gotten themselves into and if she really was cut out for the dream in her heart. She thought maybe not, but in reality she had no choice but to muster on and pretend she knew what to do. She maneuvered Henry into the car, opened the back door for Corky and Vicky to jump in too, and arranged to pick up Randy. "We're going to a motel tonight, I don't care how. And I'll take care of all this tomorrow." At least they'd all be together and warm that night.

They slept well in the motel room, medication helping ease Henry's coughing. Corky nestled in his own den under the writing desk and Vicky perched on the luggage rack. The next morning Henry stayed in bed while Luanne and Randy visited the motel's free continental breakfast. She brought back oatmeal and plenty of apple juice for Henry. By the time they returned home, Luanne was feeling stronger herself, and able to get a nice fire burning with the wood from the general store. Good thing she'd paid attention and learned how to teepee the twigs and get a substantial fire blazing. She bundled Henry into bed and piled on the blankets. His fever was gone, and he fell asleep readily.

Randy helped her scrape the melting ice and slush off the floor. Her arms ached, but she kept pushing the shovel and lugging buckets of soggy mess. After countless shovel scoops, towel wrings and mop swipes, the floor was once again visible, although filthy. She watched Randy wipe off his hands and move toward his little curtained-off area of a room. She approached him and put her arm around his shoulder. "I know," she began. "I know this can't be easy, living here. If you want to go..."

"I'm fine," he said, cutting her off. He motioned toward the big bed. "Is Henry going to be okay?"

She nodded. "He'll be okay."

"And you?"

She kissed Randy's cheek. Just having him ask erased some of the worry. "I'm going to be okay too." She crawled into the old recliner chair next to the woodstove and wrapped up in a blanket. Corky settled down by her side. The bark from a birch log snapped. Her husband was sick, the house was far from done, and winter was kicking them in the butt, but they were hanging on.

Vicky jumped up into her lap and Luanne felt the cat's soft body vibrate. A contented purr. Cats had a way of spreading serenity with just a gentle purr. They would make it. They'd all be fine. But, Luanne thought, lowering her cheek to Vicky's warm fur, spring had better hurry.

Corky, the faithful dog

Timbers await construction of a home to replace the school bus.

Luanne gives a chicken individual attention.

The pond adorns a long, winding driveway…

... that leads to a graceful Green Mountains view.

Animals Teach

Chapter 5

Spring Babies

A DETERMINED PURPLE CROCUS pushed up out of the snow. Teeny buds curled tight on tree branches, seeking the warmth of the sun to unfurl. The roads were rutted no longer with ice but with muddy potholes instead. Luanne saw her first robin tugging a worm out of the earth. Finally, spring, green grass, and warmth. Construction on the house could resume.

The dainty white cat had grown independent since kittenhood and, like many country cats, now enjoyed spending her days outside hunting. Luanne and Henry kept a window open for her to come and go. Apparently she had hunted up a boyfriend. When Luanne noticed Vicky's round belly hanging low as she slunk out the window, she clapped her hands together. This was part of the farm experience she'd always hoped for—animals, babies, new life. Once the kittens were born, she'd take Vicky to the vet to be spayed, but these babies were very much wanted.

Weeks later when Vicky went into labor, Luanne hovered by her side.

Henry leaned in. "Think she needs anything?"

"I don't know … she seems to like where I've got her all right." Luanne wanted Vicky to have a special place for nesting, but there wasn't a quiet room in the crowded basement. The best she could do was to offer an empty wooden box, lined with a soft towel and some clean newspapers. She'd read something about mother cats needing to be undisturbed during delivery and wondered what would happen if she lingered too close. "Maybe she needs privacy," Luanne suggested. But when she left, Vicky yowled, so she returned.

About an hour later, the first kitten arrived, the tiniest speck of fur Luanne had ever seen. Vicky licked her kitten gently.

"She's a good mom," Luanne said.

Before long there were four sweet kittens lined up and nursing. Only one was white like Vicky. The others, brown and gray tiger stripes, must have taken after their daddy. Luanne wondered where he was and if he'd ever know—or care—that he had offspring. Luanne watched the babies over the next several days and they seemed to be growing strong. What a wonder to have babies come into the world in the house that was, in a way, being born itself.

About a week later Luanne was washing her hands in the curtained-off area that served as the bathroom, when she heard a muffled *mew*. It sounded so close, but it couldn't be. The kittens were still too young to get out alone. She was just about to dismiss the whole thing when she heard it again. A soft, muted cry.

"Are the kittens in the box?" she called out to Henry, drying her hands as she scanned the bathroom.

"No." Henry appeared by her side. "They're not! Just Vicky."

"Do you hear that?" she asked.

They both stood quietly, tilting their heads in different directions, when the sound came again. *Mew*.

Henry dropped to his knees and crawled around the cramped bathroom. There weren't many places a kitten could hide. "Do ya think ..." He lifted aside a board in a section of the floor that had been intentionally left un-cemented in order to provide access to plumbing. The hole beneath was cold and dirty, and not a nice place for kittens.

Luanne peered into the dark space. Little eyes shined back at her.

"They're here!"

Henry reached into the cavity, gently retrieved a kitten and handed it up to her. "Are they all in there?" she asked.

One by one Henry liberated the kittens from the dark recesses under the floor. "That's only three," Luanne said.

"I don't see any more."

Luanne called to the kitten, although she was unsure how well a baby cat could actually hear. What if it was trapped? It would be so frightened in that dark, cold place. What if she had to spend her days walking around the house, hearing the sounds of a gray tiger kitten pawing the dirt under the floor, unable to get back to its mother?

"We'll tear apart the floor if we have to," Henry said.

"Wait." She brought Vicky to the edge of the hole and stroked her back. "She got them in there, she must know how to get them out." Vicky poked her face into the opening, whiskers twitching. She let out a soft plea.

Sure enough, before long a tiny pink nose appeared. Vicky poked her face into the hole and nuzzled the kitten's head. Before it could disappear again, Luanne scooped up the last kitten and put them all safely back in the proper place.

"Have you ever heard of a cat moving her kittens?" she asked her friend Barbara at work the next day.

"Oh yeah," Barbara answered. "Younger cat mothers, especially, get nervous and hide them in all sorts of weird places."

As if under the bathroom floor wasn't weird enough, the next hiding place was even worse. Luanne and Henry returned home from work one day to discover that the kittens were gone again. As Luanne was searching, Vicky wandered down from the woods.

"Vicky, where are your kittens?"

The cat rubbed up against Luanne's ankle.

"Vicky, show me your babies," Luanne asked, and this time the cat meowed, turned, and headed up into the woods. Luanne followed her to a dirty old log where all four kittens nestled amongst some ferns. She couldn't imagine why Vicky would bring the babies outdoors when they had a safe, dry living space provided for them. She picked up the kittens, cradled them in her arms, and brought them back to their box. Vicky followed reluctantly.

The next day after work, however, Luanne discovered that Vicky had moved the kittens back to the log again. "We should close the windows, keep her inside."

"She must want them there for a reason." Henry had grown up with farm animals. "We have to trust her instincts in this."

A week later Luanne and Henry were making dinner when Vicky wandered in. Luanne had been checking on the babies up in the woods every day and, although she still didn't like the arrangement, the little family seemed to be getting along okay. At that moment, however, Luanne recoiled.

"Oh no, Vicky!" She turned to Henry. "What an unearthly stink!"

Henry opened the door. "Sorry, girl. Take your skunky self back outside."

Luanne hurried out the door behind Vicky. "I'm going to make sure the kittens are okay. I hope they didn't get sprayed too."

She climbed up the woodsy hill, the odor growing stronger, and found the old log. There were only little indentations in the bed of ferns. The kittens were gone. Her heart sank. "Vicky!" she gasped. "Where are your babies?"

Vicky just sat and meowed. Luanne lifted her, despite the offensive stench, and clutched her tight. "Oh, Vicky," she cried. "The skunk got your babies." She fell to the ground and rocked the frightened mother cat.

It was all her fault. If only she'd insisted that the cats stayed inside. If only she'd watched them more carefully. "The skunk got your babies," she sobbed, "I'm so sorry."

Vicky touched her nose to Luanne's cheek and squeezed out of her arms. She trotted over to the opposite side of the log and lay down, stretching her body out facing the log. It sounded like she was pawing the mossy leaves, but when Luanne looked more closely, there were the four kittens, lined up to nurse. They were alive! Vicky must have moved them. The good mother had kept her babies safe from the skunk.

One weekend Luanne and Henry organized a work crew: Randy, his friend from school, Henry's redheaded friend Tom whom he'd met in town. Some worked on the house while others built a crude barn to shelter the animals. Just about anyone they knew ended up joining in and lending a hand at one time or another. Uncle Ward arrived to help, as he did at every possible opportunity. "Got my good work shirt on," he said as he stepped out of the car. The shirt had so many patches covering it that every time he returned from a weekend, his wife threw it away. But he'd pull it out of the trash, and she'd mend it again.

As they started gathering their tools, Luanne noticed a movement in the grass by the chicken coop. "Well, look who we have here!"

"Is that one of the kittens born up in the woods?" her uncle asked.

"Well, they weren't born there, but they seem to be living there." She crouched low and held out her palm. A gangly tiger-striped kitten approached cautiously. Vicky stood several yards back, offering neither instruction nor warning.

"How old are they?"

"About eight weeks old now." The little cat picked his way over the bumpy ground and batted a blade of grass. He walked carefully but not fearfully and sniffed Luanne's hand. "Why, you're just too curious to stay away, aren't you?" she said. "You're a little Curious George."

The next day the kitten returned with a smaller, smoky colored cat by its side. The smaller kitten's gray tail stuck out straight like a railroad spike. "George and Spiky," Luanne decided. They looked plump and healthy. "Good job." She stroked Vicky's head and then turned to Uncle Ward. Since the kittens were old enough to leave their mother, Luanne thought she ought to find them homes. "Wouldn't you like to take a kitten home with you?"

"Tempting," he said. "But I'm allergic."

The only girl, with long white fur like her mama, was easy to place. A gray angora went to Barbara, her friend from school. No one claimed George and Spiky. "You didn't try very hard," said Henry. It was true. They'd already claimed her.

Chapter 6

The Pond

HER EARLIEST DREAMS of a home always featured a glistening pond, so much so that it figured more prominently than the house. The water always gleamed with the most spectacular shade of blue, clear and deep, and atop swam a pair of swans with their necks bent the way they show in inspirational cards, forming the shape of the perfect heart.

In reality, their pond was lopsided and murky. It looked as if some giant passing through had left a haphazard footprint that then filled with muddy water. Still, Luanne was anxious for some sort of life to abide there.

The school year ended and Luanne was off work for the summer. Cleaning out her classroom, she realized she had to do something with the aquarium of goldfish she'd been keeping there. When no one else agreed to take it for the summer, she asked a janitor to help carry it to her car.

She drove home, careful not to hit too many bumps, and stopped at the bottom of the driveway. Henry was done with his cleaning jobs early and had started hoeing the lower garden. He came over and looked into the back of the car where an aquarium rested on the floor.

"Goldfish can survive in a pond, right?" she asked. She'd heard of koi ponds. This couldn't be much different.

"Don't see why not," Henry answered.

Together they hefted the aquarium and dumped the tankful—three orange fish, three orange and-white, each about two inches long, into the pond. The fish slipped out of the clear water into the muddy pond. As the last little one wriggled over the aquarium edge, Luanne's mind captured it there midair, frozen in time—each scale shimmering in the sun, its buggy eyes flashing with goldfish vacancy—yet she asked herself if maybe the poor fishy soul wondered why it had to leave its home, where all was comfortable and familiar, and go into this huge pond that was so dark and cold. For a moment she even tried to snatch it back, nearly dropping her side of the tank as she shot out one hand toward the gold. But it was too late; the tiny fish disappeared into the murk.

After that, she stopped at the bottom of the driveway and looked at the pond every time she passed, silently scanning the water. She never spotted the fish. When not even a ripple broke the surface of the water, she'd slowly make her way up the rest of the driveway.

The first ducks to reside in the pond were two beautiful domestic mallards. Luanne and Henry paused from work on the house and called to them, "Quack, quack."

The ducks answered back, "Quack! Quack! Quack!"

Luanne felt giddy with happiness. "We can talk to ducks!"

Shortly after the mallards arrived, a neighbor across town offered them some ducks for free. These were not the beautiful white ducks Luanne was familiar with, but large fowl with mostly black bodies and white splotches, as if a bucket of paint had tipped over on top of them. Their heads were small with warty-looking necks blotched with red turkey skin.

Luanne learned that their name, Muscovy, meant "from the Moscow area," although the ducks weren't really from Moscow. They were native to Mexico and South America.

The mallards flapped out of the way as the new clan waddled out of their wooden box and splashed into the pond, paddling along its muddy banks. If they didn't exactly add to the beauty of the place, they did seem somehow fitting to the disheveled state of things.

In addition to lacking the beauty of their domestic cousins, the Muscovies were also quackless. Quackless, but not silent. Instead, they made a dreadful hissing sound. Sometimes they are called Whispering Ducks. Luanne listened to their hiss-whispering and felt sad that they weren't able to communicate without straining their voices in such a harsh way.

A week or so later, Henry came home from work with a big, unwieldy cardboard container. Luanne wondered if he'd driven all the way from town with that box on his lap. The grin on his face widened as Luanne watched a fat white goose push her head out of the box.

"Henry, where on earth did you get that goose?" Luanne asked, dropping the bucket of chicken feed to check out the new arrival. The goose was enormous, flogging the sides of the box with its wings.

"The lady didn't want her."

"What lady?"

"No idea. I just saw her on the side of the road with this goose making an awful fuss, so I pulled over and stopped. I thought she was trying to chase it off, so I asked, 'Is that your goose?' And she replied 'Yes, but I sure wish it wasn't.' That ol' lady was chasing her with a broom, and the goose was carrying on and flapping and honking and being all ornery and…"

"So of course you thought we should have her."

"Why not?"

Luanne tried to look stern, but couldn't hold back a smile. The goose was pretty cute.

"She said that she got the goose for her grandkids," Henry explained, "but she didn't have a pond. And the grandkids were terrified of the goose anyway. Whenever they were out in the yard and the goose came anywhere near, they ran back into the house shrieking. The lady was only too happy to give her to me when I offered. I said we'd give her a nice home and a big pond."

"Well, that we have. Should we take her down?"

Henry couldn't carry the heavy, squirming box all the way back down the driveway, so he tipped it over, which caused the goose to run, honking and flapping even more. When she stretched her neck and hissed, Henry only laughed. "Git down to the pond, Gertie!"

"Gertie?" Luanne asked.

"Why not?" Henry shrugged.

Corky ran over to help with the herding, but the goose proved too intimidating for him and he backed off, following from a safe distance. Luanne and Henry chased her down the steep hill. A few times she lifted off, fluttering a few feet off the ground, and Luanne worried she might fly away, but she didn't seem adept in aeronautic maneuvers. When at last they reached the edge of the pond, Gertie stopped short.

"Okay," said Henry. "Here ya go. Home sweet home."

The irritable goose looked back at him, as if to say he'd made some sort of terrible mistake. She didn't seem interested in joining the ducks in the pond. She tried to waddle away. Henry and Luanne chased her down. Henry faked her out with a quick hop-turn and snatched her up.

"You've got a pond now, Gertie," he coaxed. He hefted her to the edge of the pond and gently tossed her into the water. She shrieked, flapping as if she'd been tossed into hot lava, and skedaddled back out.

"Geese like water," he said.

Not this goose, she seemed to say.

Once again Henry caught her and tossed her a little farther out. Gertie honked angrily and again, half-swam/half-flew back out.

One more time, Henry cornered her and sent her back into the pond, careful not to hurt her, this time as far toward the middle as he could. "You'll like it!" he assured.

Gertie wasted no time. She spun around in midair, stuck her neck forward, and headed back to the shore, whipping her feet so fast that she actually ran on top of the water! Henry and Luanne collapsed on the ground laughing. That was the end of swimming lessons for the day.

Gertie didn't readily take to the water, but she did find a different interest. Henry. When Henry worked in the garden, there was his waddling shadow staring at him and honking gently. Whenever Henry drove up the driveway, Gertie ran out to greet him and then followed him around step for step. One time when Henry was pitching hay in the chicken coop, Luanne discovered the goose on the roof, impatiently waiting for Henry to come back out. She'd obviously forgiven him for throwing her in the pond and perhaps even was grateful to him for rescuing her from the scary grandchildren who shrieked in the backyard.

Gertie, however, wasn't fond of Luanne. Maybe it was because she took her eggs, but Luanne reasoned it was more likely because she stood between Gertie and her true love, Henry.

Since Gertie seemed to have so much love to give, Luanne and Henry decided to get her a mate. They came home with a gander, a lovely fellow with bright eyes and a bold strut. Gertie took one look at him and ran behind Henry. The gander engaged in friendly chase, but Gertie kept her distance and never let him get too close. When he approached while she was with Henry, she'd hide and look up as if to say "Get. That. Thing. Away from me."

Each night they shut Gertie and the gander into the barn to keep them safe. Eventually she saw the benefit of snuggling next to a warm body and finally accepted her feathered boyfriend.

And eventually, she also took to water. One day Luanne was scattering food for the ducks and sprinkled a little right in the pond. Gertie ate her way to the edge. Luanne barely moved, trying not to frighten her off. The goose splashed into the water, swam around a little, and then stepped gingerly out as if it had been no big deal. Luanne tried not to make a big deal out of it either, but she smiled thinking that their funny feathered friend finally felt like this was home.

As she was preparing to head back up to the house, Henry and Randy drove down to the pond, a little wooden structure perched on the back of the garden tractor. She recognized it as something Randy had built that year in woodshop.

"What are you doing with Corky's doghouse?" Luanne asked. There was always something unusual happening, so she wasn't truly surprised.

"He never uses it!" Randy said, unloading the little house from the tractor. And so the dog house became a duck house. Luanne hoped it would help all the birds feel more secure, especially if there were to be babies. A little improvisation—maybe that was the trick to making things easier on the farm. A little improvisation, and a little faith. How much faith would it take, she wondered, to be sure that everything would be okay.

FAITH

There were no cats in the orphanage, but one time Luanne left the home for a weekend visit to Grammie Worth and her black-and-white cat, Mittens.

Mittens was the biggest, fattest cat Luanne had ever seen. The most remarkable thing about Mittens was his huge, white feet. When he sat on the stool in the kitchen, his paws spread out across the front, an extra furry toe hanging over each edge. Luanne loved to take a string of yarn from Grammie's knitting and dangle it in front of Mittens, just so she could watch those enormous paws bat at the yarn.

Grammie Worth stepped out from the pantry, a sparkle of sugar on her plump cheek. The kitchen smelled of cinnamon and vanilla. "Has Mittens always been your cat, Grammie?" Luanne asked.

"Since a tiny kitten."

"You mean, he's never had another mother?" Luanne assumed that everyone had several mothers, as she had.

"Just his cat mother."

"What happened to his cat mother? Did she die?"

"Oh no, nothing happened to his cat mother. She lived with a big family in a big old house, as I recall. That mama cat had at least a dozen kittens. They couldn't keep them all. So I went over there and saw this little one jumping around like a flea in a mitten. Right then and there I knew he was mine."

"Didn't the kitten mind when you took him away?" Luanne put her hand on the cat's giant paw.

"Oh no, he didn't mind at all. Didn't hardly know any difference. That's the way it is with animals. They don't stay with their real mama for long."

"Well, how'd you know he'd be happy here with you?"

"Oh, child, I don't know. God willing, he's happy here. I take good care of him, love him. You know, child, we can only do our best and the rest is up to the Lord. I've seen my share of hard times. Lost your Grampa more than fifteen years ago, lost a brother in the war, lived with and lived without. I never much figured I had any control over any of it."

"Who does?"

"It's all in His hands." Grammie looked heavenward.

Luanne wasn't sure who the mysterious "he" was who apparently lived upstairs, although she'd never seen him. But she did know a little bit about God, because she heard Grammie praying before bed, before a meal, or even when she was just sitting and knitting.

"Do prayers work?" Luanne asked once.

"Not like you think they do," Grammie said. "But they work."

Why was God such a mysterious puzzle? Luanne pushed her chair back and went out to the yard to play. The clouds hung dark and heavy, ready to burst open. The Black River trickled along the edge of the backyard, and Luanne wandered to where Grammie kept four fat white ducks.

Luanne knew enough to stay on the grassy side of the water. River rats skittered about near the oozy mud, their fat bodies disappearing into holes in the earth, long, bald tails following like strands of spaghetti. She wasn't afraid of the rats, but one day she'd seen something terrible. Halfway down one of the rat holes was the back end of a duck, limp legs dangling at its side. Luanne's stomach had twisted like a towel in Grammie's wringer washing machine. If God loved every creature, why would He have allowed that to happen? The poor, innocent duck didn't deserve such a horrible death.

Before long, the wind picked up and fat raindrops fell. The sky darkened in an instant. Luanne headed for the house just as Grammie opened the back door. "Hurry!" Grammie called over a huge clap of thunder. Mittens whisked out from nowhere and darted out the door.

"Mittens! Come back!" Grammie yelled.

Luanne tried to catch the cat, but he hid under a shrub by the maple tree.

"You get inside," Grammie said, "I'm going to get my umbrella."

"Mittens is scared," Luanne said, cringing as thunder crashed again.

Grammie opened the umbrella and ran outside, rain now pelting the ground in angry torrents. Luanne watched from the kitchen door. "God, if you are real, help Grammie to get Mittens back," she whispered.

Then came the loudest crash of thunder she ever heard. An electric flash of light. A bolt shot down from the sky directly to a broad limb of the tree. Grammie flung the umbrella, grabbed the cat by the scruff of the neck and shot back into the house. "Hold the door! We're coming!" she called, just as the huge branch crashed to the ground behind her.

Grammie snatched up a towel, wrapped Mittens, and then carried him back to the bedroom and flopped onto the feather bed. Whenever Luanne had climbed onto the soft mattress, her tiny body made only a slight dent. Grammie, however, sank deep into the feathers, the sides rising up and swallowing her whole.

"C'mon," Grammie said, and Luanne joined her and Mittens. Grammie pulled a wool blanket around their shoulders. "We'll keep each other warm," she said. Luanne hugged Mittens and his giant paws. Grammie hugged Luanne. She felt very brave and safe for the rest of the storm, snuggled between Grammie's soft body and the warm cat. Her prayer was answered and Mittens was back safely, although she thought God really needn't have caused such a commotion first.

Chapter 7

Raise the Roof

HAMMERS, ROUTERS, LEVELS, a table saw, window frames, work gloves, and tool belts littered the ground, with chickens running around atop it all. Rows of logs progressed upward as Luanne and Henry settled the grooves into place and drove in ten-inch spikes. A huge work crew, led by Uncle Ward, gathered to help. Luanne made egg salad and whipped up sandwiches for everyone. "And we've got to offer everyone beer," Henry said, filling a cooler.

She felt a little warning twist of her stomach when he said it. Henry seemed to have a beer quite often. Too often? She'd never really seen him drunk, at least not angry drunk. Just mellow, until he fell asleep in the chair. But maybe he was right. Most men did like a cold one when they were working hard. "Just don't have too much," she said. "We don't want you falling off the roof."

The roof was the project for the day. At last! Each row of logs fitted together, shorter and shorter until they reached a peak, like a child's Lincoln Logs toy of old. Then, a huge carrying beam would be placed from end to end to support the planks for the roof.

They needed everyone's hands to help place the carrying beam. Eighteen feet long and heavy as a bull moose, the beam needed to be raised ten feet up to the rafters. Uncle Ward directed the job. Randy stood below with a pulley rope to lift the beam inch by inch. "Don't let go!" Luanne urged. She steadied a ladder for Tom, who was helping steer the beam into place. The ladder shook.

"Are you cold?"

"To tell you the truth," Tom replied, tugging his Budweiser cap down over his red hair, "I'm terrified. If this thing slips ..."

Luanne didn't feel so secure herself. A few weeks earlier they'd been placing a log near the peak of the ceiling. Henry was at the top of the ladder. When Luanne handed him the log, it slipped from his grip and clocked her on top of the head. She'd sprawled on the floor, seeing stars. Henry jumped down from the ladder in one leap, terrified that he'd knocked her out. But in a few minutes she was up again, and they got the job done.

That log, however, hadn't been as large as the one they were dealing with now. This one took six people to maneuver. If any one of them slipped, the log would crash down and heaven help anyone below. Henry perched astride the top rafters. Did he think he was a strapping young dude, rather than a slightly out-of-shape, balding, middle-aged man? But he never slowed down or acted his age. Hopefully he had enough confidence for both of them.

The beam swayed precariously. Uncle Ward helped Randy raise the pulley rope, their arms shaking. Tom guided the heavy log. Henry reached out to hitch the end in place. After three hours, they finally secured the beam. A huge cheer went up from the workers.

"It's beautiful!" Luanne shouted out.

"At last." Henry wiped his brow.

They celebrated the rest of the day. Placing the beam meant they'd soon be able to build a roof, and the roof meant that they'd finally be able to move out of the basement. A roof meant that their "weekend project" would be nearing completion, at least the outside structure. A roof meant that they'd be able to concentrate more on the animals and gardens, like in her dreams.

One of the animals of her dreams was a donkey. Luanne brought the subject up with Henry in the barn one day. "We've got this stall here," she said. "Kinda looks like it needs filling up."

"With what?" Henry asked, spreading a forkful of hay on the floor.

"Well…," she said, "I saw a sign. Donkeys for sale. I always wanted a donkey. They were roaming about in that field up the road, so sweet. Big ears. Big eyes. Don't you think we need a donkey?"

"*Need?*" asked Henry, his expression playful. Of course, when it came to bringing home animals, he was never one to resist. He smiled broadly. "Do *you* think we need a donkey?"

The next weekend their new furry friend joined the family. He was solidly built, soft, gray, with a beautiful dark cross on his back. "I'll remember to pray whenever I see him," she said. And at first she prayed with gratitude for finally having a pet donkey. "I've been asking God for a donkey for so long!" They named him Dr. Seuss, fixed him up a snug stall, and gave him food and water.

Then, they were all settled in for the night when they heard a loud screech followed by a low bellow. "What is that horrible noise?" Henry asked. "It's worse than squeaky wheels on a freight train."

Hee hawww hee hawwww.

"Maybe he's just lonely," Luanne considered, pulling a pillow over her head. The noise continued night after night. So then the prayer changed. She sent up a plea for Dr. Seuss to stop braying at night.

Henry fixed him up with plenty of hay, food and water. Luanne stroked his neck and talked sweetly to him, but he shuffled in his stall uneasily. Luanne backed away. Was he upset? Lonely? Sick? She opened his stall and tried to coax him outside. He kicked, just missing her leg. She didn't think he meant to be malicious, but it startled her.

She and Henry lay in bed every night, listening to the donkey's plaintive calls, braying at the moon.

"He's not getting any exercise," Henry said. "We don't have a big enough barn for him to run around in."

"And it looks like his hooves need trimming," Luanne added. "I don't know if we can do a donkey's hooves. The sheep are difficult enough."

"Do you think we need to brush his teeth?" Henry asked. "They look mighty yellow."

Heee hawwww.

Luanne stared out the window at the soft glow in the night sky. Dr. Seuss wasn't happy. Who'd have thought it would be so difficult to understand a little donkey's needs? She had to admit, they were out of their league. As much as she loved him and his gentle, soulful eyes, this was no place for him. The next day she fed him a bag of carrots, hugged his soft neck, and returned him to the farm.

Sometimes it was right for God not to give you everything you asked for.

Scaffolding replaced ladders as Henry lugged heavy loads of shingles up to the top of the house. Vicky scurried up the scaffolds, but Corky stayed below, crying pitifully whenever Luanne climbed up, because he wanted so to be beside her. She left the highest work to the others, because when she climbed too high the ground went spinning. Henry walked across the roof with ease, but Randy's knuckles turned white as he hung over the edge. Summer faded into fall and the days grew dark earlier. Luanne lit the lantern so they could get in a few more hours' work. By the time frost laced the morning ground and they could see their breath in the air, the roof was nearly complete.

One chilly night Henry started a fire in the woodstove. In the morning, he woke up feeling slightly nauseous but pulled on his quilted flannel coat to drive into town. Luanne got ready slowly, feeling lightheaded but thinking she'd be able to go to work. Randy, too, said that he felt ill.

"Maybe you'd better stay home from school," Luanne said. "Something must be going around. Must be we all picked up a bug. I'll check in on you at lunchtime."

Throughout the morning she started to feel better, but she couldn't concentrate on work. Something didn't feel right. She had to get home—she couldn't wait until lunchtime. She arranged to leave work early.

When she arrived home, Corky was pacing down by the end of the driveway, circling the pond. He followed her car up the hill, but kept a distance from the house. Henry was already back and standing outside with Randy, wrapped in a blanket. She rushed out of the car to their sides.

"He said he woke up feeling really sick and disoriented," Henry explained.

"What happened?"

"The room was full of smoke," Randy choked. "I almost didn't find the door."

"Smoke!" she gasped. "Was there a fire?" She didn't see any damage from the outside. "Are you okay?" She helped Randy sit down in the car and turned on the heater.

"I think it was the chimney." Henry had vented the woodstove's chimney out a basement window, but apparently as the work on the house progressed, the pipe was no longer tall enough to vent properly. "Everything backed up into the house." Henry shook his head.

Luanne put her arm around Randy, watching the color slowly return to his ashen face. It struck her, then, that they could all have carbon monoxide poisoning. The poisonous, odorless gas probably seeped back into the house with all that smoke. How many times had she read about families succumbing to such poison, never even aware of the danger permeating their home? It could have been them. She couldn't stop her body from trembling. If Randy hadn't found his way out, if Henry hadn't been there, if she hadn't come home early...

Henry turned away, walking slowly toward the barn. Luanne frowned. "Where are you going?"

"I'm just..." His guilty face gave him away. She'd happened upon some of his "secret hiding places" before. She knew he was heading out to get a drink.

"Don't, Henry."

"Don't what?" He turned, his face reddening. "I'm just going to see if we have more stovepipe. I'm going to put that chimney right up through the ceiling the way it should have been in the first place." He stomped away.

Maybe Henry needed his beer to get through the endless work, exhaustion and stress. They all needed something. She closed the passenger door and went around to the driver's side. "I'm taking Randy out for a drive," she called, "and we're not coming back until that chimney's done!" Maybe her anger was misdirected, but she couldn't help it. They'd put everyone in harm's way, all for a crazy dream to build this house themselves, to have a farm and feel as close as possible to God's green earth. Corky jumped into the car with them, but Vicky took off into the woods. Animals were smart. They knew when to stand by you, like Corky. But they also

116

knew when it was time to turn tail and run. Maybe she should listen to Vicky.

She drove down the long driveway. "Feeling better?" she asked Randy.

"Getting there."

She stopped at the end of the drive before turning onto the dirt road. A motion by the pond caught her attention. At first she thought it was just a glint of sunlight playing tricks on her. Then she saw a ripple. Then another. She glanced over at Randy. "Do you see what I see?"

There, breaking the surface of the pond, a goldfish jumped. Several more wriggled nearby. But not just the six she'd emptied into the pond at the beginning of the summer. There were dozens. No, there must have been more than a hundred! The water was bursting with them, in every color combination possible: all gold; gold and white; gold and black; white with black; all black; gold, white and black all together. And they weren't tiny aquarium fish any longer either. They were eight, ten, twelve inches long, shimmering gold flecks in the sun, fan tails swooshing in the water. She wanted to say something profound but no words came. All she knew was the feeling of awe that filled her as she watched those fish. Although she had dumped them into a murky pond, not knowing what to expect, they had survived.

Chapter 8

Loftiness

"I'D LIKE TO make the last payment on the woodstove," Luanne said, opening her checkbook on the store counter. They'd selected the soapstone model last year and she was beginning to think she'd never get to see it outside the showroom.

"Where would you like that delivered?" The shop owner rubbed his stubbled chin and scribbled in a notepad. When Luanne gave him the address, his eyes widened with recognition. "Oh, you're the crazy, err...the people who have been living in the basement up there on the hill!"

"Yes, we're the crazy people," Luanne sighed, smiling.

"I don't know how you're doing it, but at least now you're going to get yourself a good stove. One of our most popular models. Keep you nice and warm."

"Actually, we're moving upstairs now!" Luanne could barely believe it even as the words came out. "We don't have floors or interior walls or much else, but we have a new kitchen and a bathroom. We've got a bunch of furniture out of storage and once we get this stove, we'll have just about everything."

"Don't you worry, ma'am," the man said, smiling. "We'll bring it on over this afternoon. I think you've waited long enough."

Luanne had always said that all she needed was a roof over her head, but she never knew just how much that meant until they moved upstairs. The main floor was spacious and open. She tilted her head; she could see all the way up to the rafters and the huge carrying beam that had taken the workers all day to install. She ran her hand along the log walls. The floors weren't finished, but at least they were plywood instead of cement. There was still much more work to be done, but she was proud of what they'd accomplished. Log by log, through sickness and health, rain and snow, day after day, by the sweat of their brows. A real log house in the country. She looked out their very own window at the sweeping mountain view that years earlier she'd proclaimed reason enough to purchase the imperfect land, and nodded.

That night, however, she climbed the shaky ladder to their loft bedroom. Henry snored soundly, but she wrestled with sleep. The openness mocked her. The tight space of the basement with everyone hemmed in so close meant she knew they were all still together. This space, so gaping and vulnerable, could never protect her like that solid, cement fortress. Whatever peril lay ahead would have no trouble finding her here. She gazed up. They'd placed those logs up there, but what did they know? She tried to push back the thought that the huge carrying beam could come crashing down and crush her alive on her bed.

In the morning, everything looked better again. She rubbed her eyes and set her feet down on the bare floorboards. They'd not yet built a railing at the top of the loft and it would only take one tiny slip for an unexpected, painful landing. Looking down at the open space below, her stomach flip-flopped. No, she didn't want to go back to living in the basement. She just didn't want to fall and break her neck.

As she lingered in that world of half-awake, a rap at the window sent her shooting back for the covers.

"What was that?" She shook Henry.

"What?"

"Someone's knocking on the window!"

"How could anyone be knocking on the window way up here?" Henry yawned.

True. The window was twenty feet off the ground. It wasn't like someone could have just happened to be passing by. She got up and peered out. Maybe it was just a branch or something. As she pulled her sweatshirt over her head, however, she heard it again. A light but definite thump against the glass. As she scratched her head, a white paw appeared from above. *Rap! Rap! Rap!* The paw swatted against the pane. Then a furry face and whiskers peeked over. Vicky was up on the roof, hanging over the edge as if to say "Would ya puh-leez let me in?"

Luanne laughed. Randy's bedroom was downstairs. He must have gotten up early and let the cat outside and then gone back to bed. Vicky loved to scurry up a ladder, still leaning against the side of the house, and crawl around up on the roof. "Okay, I'm coming to let you in." Luanne said. "Get back down from there!"

Luanne pulled on warm slacks and socks and backed down the loft ladder. Corky, who couldn't manage scaling the ladder, awakened and slobbered Luanne's ankles as soon as they were in reach.

As she started a pot of coffee, Corky went outside and Vicky came inside. Randy and Henry woke up just as Luanne was taking her basket to the henhouse. She delighted that she could simply take a few steps and collect their own fresh eggs for breakfast. She opened the coop and the chickens scurried out. "Good morning, ladies." She bent and ruffled their backs as they waddled past. "Aren't you in a hurry! Aren't you feisty today!" She loved talking to the animals. "Look at your pretty feathers!" And then, especially for Corky, "Do you know how much I love you?" She threw him a stick, but he only chased it for a few feet and then returned. More important that he stay close by. How did she get so lucky as to deserve such devotion? She bent down and hugged his neck. She'd do anything for him. She just hoped she was capable of giving the animals as much as they gave her.

NURTURE

For her seventh grade English oral report, Luanne had read, "I learned about reproduction through experience." All the students in the room burst out laughing. Her cheeks blazed when she realized her mistake. But it was true. She'd learned a lot from her grandmother's birds.

The summer of her eleventh birthday, Luanne's grandmother, her father's mother, had picked her up from the orphanage and brought her back to live with her. Mommie Johnson had never agreed with her son's decision to send Luanne to Kurn Hattin.

She'd stayed out of things for as long as she could, considering it improper to meddle with someone else's parenting. But enough was enough.

Luanne loved Mommie's huge, sprawling house on Wall Street. (Springfield's Wall Street, unlike New York's, was a small-town residential road on a steep hill.) There was a three-car garage, beautiful gardens, trellises, redwood patio furniture, a wraparound porch and best of all, a house full of animals—Chili Bean the big black cat, Cameo the Cocker Spaniel, Nicker the Maltese. And hundreds of birds.

Even though Luanne woke up early, Mommie was always already up and working, a clean apron over her outfit, her auburn hair in a bun. She always smelled of White Shoulders cologne—the sweetest scent Luanne ever knew.

Mommie housed boarders in the spare bedrooms, cooked meals, and took in laundry. When Luanne came home from school, Mommie was still at work. Luanne never knew anyone to work as hard as Mommie. Trouble was, Mommie worked so diligently, she expected everyone else to do the same. Luanne often found herself the recipient of chores when Mommie thought she'd been too idle. Luanne made beds, swept floors, and peeled potatoes. But Mommie never asked her to work harder than she worked herself.

After school one day, Luanne stepped into the kitchen and set down her books. The hot smell of steam from the flat iron mingled with the aroma of fresh baked bread. Mommie slid a crisp men's dress shirt onto a hanger and set it aside. The cat curled under the ironing board. Luanne picked up little Nicker and gave him a hug and kiss. It was easy to tell how much he adored her. His whole body wriggled with delight.

"Better go tend to those birds," Mommie greeted.

"Yes," Luanne answered, setting down the dog and turning toward the cellar stairs.

"Wait," Mommie said.

Luanne paused.

"Where's *my* hug and kiss?"

Luanne smiled and wrapped herself around her grandmother's stout frame.

She raced down the stairs two at a time to the bird room. Mommie raised parakeets and Luanne helped, which is how she came to write her English report on reproduction. The business, called the

Bird Cage, had become rather well known, with clients from Alaska to Japan.

A ruckus of chirps and tweets greeted her. The aviary was big and sunny, with an attached screened porch where Mommie often let the birds fly free. The knotty-pine walls were lined with dozens of nesting boxes. On either side of the room stood towering ceiling-to-floor cages—one for the female parakeets, one for the males. Luanne watched them perch on the swings and hop along the bottom wires. Each one was a different color, pastel and beautiful. Solid yellow. Violet. Light green with a yellow head. Aqua blue with a white head. White and gray. Prettier than the lineup in a candy shop window.

Luanne scooped a cup of birdseed and filled the little metal cups. The parakeets fluttered to her hand. It never ceased to thrill her, every time she walked in the room, how the birds stirred and flew about, enthusiastic for her company. In return, she loved to supply nourishment for them. Although there were, at times—depending upon the season and how many babies were born—more than a hundred parakeets, she made an effort to notice them all as individuals. Which one always sat on the swing, which one liked to look in the mirror, which one kept to itself. She opened the door and let a few of them out to play. She'd named one Bobbie because of its stubby bobbed tail. She sat on the floor and let Bobbie climb all over her and perch on her shoulder until it was time for her to go upstairs and help with dinner. Later in the evening she'd return, make sure they were all okay, and shut off the light.

In addition to parakeets, Mommie kept certain special birds as her favorites. One was Quito, a Cuban parrot. The little bird was predominately bright green, the color of an avocado. Scarlet red flashed at its throat and its little hooked beak.

One day Mommie received a call from the fire department instructing her to meet them at a field at the curve of the road by the river.

"Luanne, hurry, come with me," she called.

"Why? What's going on?"

"I have no idea but we have to hurry. The fire department called!"

Luanne and Mommie rushed down the road. A throng of neighbors stood, staring up a tree. Luanne heard a desperate cry. "Mother! Mmmother!"

The crowd gasped. "We thought a child was up there," a man said, wiping his brow with a handkerchief.

The cries grew more intense. "Mo-oo-ooo-therrrr!"

A fireman approached. "Someone suggested that may be one of yours." He pointed to a high branch. Luanne could make out a tiny speck of green.

"Quito!" Mommie gasped.

The poor little parrot sounded so afraid. It had never been away from home before.

"One of the boarders must have left the kitchen door open again," Mommie told Luanne.

"Will he fly down to you?" Luanne asked.

Mommie called his name. She whistled. Quito cried.

The firemen dispersed the crowd. Luanne ran home and returned with some seed and a cage. Eventually Quito returned to Mommie, who tucked him under her chin and scolded him, however sweetly, all the way home.

The most remarkable bird Mommie ever owned was a double yellow-headed Amazon parrot. A large bird, Toy was nearly sixty years old and had an expansive verbal repertoire when she bought him. Mommie lifted his cage into the backseat of the car and slid into the front seat.

As Luanne got in the back, the bird began to squawk.

"Help! Help!" cried Toy.

"What are you doing to that bird?" Mommie asked.

"Nothing!" Luanne tried to steady the cage.

"Help! Help!" The bird's voice was amazingly human. He sounded like a small boy who was crying out in terror. Passersby slowed and stared.

"Hurry up and close the door before a cop comes by and thinks we're hurting someone!" Mommie turned the key and stepped on the gas.

Toy was Mommie's favorite. Whenever Mommie took him out of the cage and carried him around on her shoulder, he was sweet and docile. But when Luanne walked into the room he cried, "Help, help!"

Most days after school Luanne practiced her trumpet in the living room. A voice called out from the kitchen. "Shut up! Shut up, right now!" She dropped her music and stomped into the kitchen, hands on her hips. No one was there except for Toy.

If he could have, he would have put his wings over his ears. He raced around in agitated circles in his cage. "Shut up! Shut up!"

One day Luanne passed Toy's cage in the kitchen. "Hellooo," Toy called sweetly. Luanne smiled and approached the cage. Maybe he wanted to be friends after all. She reached her hand toward the parrot.

Snap! Toy lunged at her with his beak.

Luanne jumped back, her heart racing. That beak was sharp and capable of some nasty damage. But more than that, her feelings were hurt. "Toy! How could you?" she said, turning from the room. As she left, Toy let out an evil laugh. "Heh heh heh hehhhhh."

To Mommie, however, Toy behaved like an angel. Mommie walked around with the parrot on her shoulder and he sang to her. "Roll out the barrel...," he crooned, trilling his r's. Mommie stroked his neck and fed him a grape.

When it was warm, Luanne took Toy's cage out on the porch. One day she sat with him, reading a book on the steps. At the sight of a couple pushing a baby carriage, Toy started crying just like an infant. When a young woman walked by, Toy let out a loud wolf whistle. The woman looked up and wrinkled her brow.

"It was the parrot," Luanne called, pointing to the cage. "Honest!" The woman hurried on.

"Don't do that to me again," Luanne scolded.

Toy practiced his scales and sang the "Beer Barrel Polka."

Finally he made the sound of a loud and amazingly realistic siren. The boarders came running down from upstairs. "What's going on?!" they gasped. Then they saw Toy.

"Heh heh heh hehhhhh," Toy laughed.

Luanne brought Toy inside. "Help! Help!" he cried.

Despite his pranks, Mommie never tired of talking with Toy and teaching him words, calculating that he could say more than four hundred. His intelligence amazed visitors. "What does the doggy say?" Mommie asked.

"Woof woof!" answered Toy.

"What does the great big dog say?"

Toy deepened his bark. "Woof, woof."

"And what does the little tiny doggy say?"

"Yip yip yip," Toy responded.

"Give me a kiss," she said, and Toy responded with a loud kissing noise.

Then Mommie turned to Luanne. "Better go tend to those birds."

Luanne turned to go take care of her responsibilities.

"Wait," Mommie said.

Luanne paused.

"Where's my hug and kiss?"

Luanne embraced her grandmother. She felt wholly nurtured, and wholly loved. She skipped downstairs to the Bird Room. The birds fluttered as if happy to see her. Not just because she fed them, she thought. They weren't just small and insignificant creatures. She would do her best to make sure they felt loved.

The log home is constructed with long timbers fitted together, building upward row by row.

*Henry's orange garden tractor has
many functions on the farm.*

*Luanne scales the scaffolding but doesn't
quite dare climb onto the roof.*

Animals Forgive

Chapter 9

Circle of Life

THE SHEEP CAME from a woman down the road after wild dogs attacked the rest of her flock. The pigs were given to them by a cousin. Henry had purchased three goats because he thought they'd clear out the lower acre and he wouldn't have so much to mow. And *everyone* seemed to drop off their unwanted chickens and ducks. These were often gifts children received for Easter and then forgot about. The farm was filling up with animals, just the way Luanne had always dreamed. Something else, however, was changing.

"I, um, I hope you understand," Randy said, hefting a log and stacking it up with the firewood. "I'm thinking of moving in with Dad. You know, the house is done. Sort of. And, you know, the city … it has a lot of advantages."

Luanne's heart hurt. Randy had graduated from high school in June but she hadn't really considered that he might leave. He never complained about anything: the cold, the heat, the work, the shabby school bus. She'd always wanted to give her children a loving home, a place where they would feel wanted and needed forever. But he was a young man now. She had to let him go.

"Dad said he could get me a job," Randy added. He finished stacking the wood. "I think it would be good."

"Of course," Luanne said, swallowing hard. "I understand."

After Randy moved out, Uncle Ward visited and helped enlarge the barn and build another shelter and enclosure down by the pond for livestock. The latest addition was two big, fat pigs. "What are you naming these two?" he asked. "Fred and Ginger?"

"We're not naming them." Henry closed the pen door. "Remember, they're supposed to be for meat."

Luanne frowned. The porkers wiggled their curly tails. "We have to call them something," she said. "We can't just say 'hey you.'"

"If we have to call them anything," Henry conceded, "it's Porkchop and Hambone. That way you'll always remember what they are destined to be."

"But ..."

"Now don't get too attached to them. Bacon is good."

Luanne gave the pigs a scratch on the head and then turned to follow Henry up the hill. They'd agreed they wanted to raise as much food of their own as possible. Until then, it had mostly been vegetables from the garden, eggs, and a few chickens. But now there were pigs. And the next day, Henry pulled in the driveway with a young white heifer. "Don't get too attached," he said again.

"C'm here, Snowflake," she called.

"Snowflake?"

"We've got to call her something." Henry started to open his mouth, but she stopped him. "And it's not going to be Sirloin Steak."

Henry built a trough for the pigs down by the road. They never had a problem keeping it full, as the cafeteria ladies gave Luanne a ten-gallon bucket of scraps, vegetables, and food the kids threw away at the end of school every day.

One day, she and Henry were on their way into town and about halfway down the driveway, looking at the pigs happily pushing their greedy noses into the slop, when Luanne noticed a small, reddish animal alongside them.

"Henry! What's that in the pigpen?"

He peered down the hill. "It looks like a fox."

"Will he hurt the pigs?" Luanne asked.

"Not likely," Henry replied. "The pigs outweigh him. Besides, why would he want to work for a meal when he has an easy supply in the trough?"

"Check it out, he's wearing a collar. And a tag. Could he be someone's pet?" Before they could get a close look the fox took off, alerted by the sound of the approaching tires.

The next day the fox returned, so they called the fish and game warden. By the time the white truck with the state emblem pulled up, the fox had run off again.

"Folks I know rescued a fox," the warden said, scanning the ground for prints. "Caught in some barbed wire. They got it medical attention, but then it got away. Must be the one."

"Did it have a tag?" Luanne asked.

"Yep," the warden replied. "The vet gave it a rabies shot, so that was a tag letting people know."

"Is he safe, do you think? With the animals?"

"I doubt he'd hurt these big ol' swine. But you don't want him wandering up there by the henhouse. Don't know a fox alive who'd turn down a chicken dinner."

"What can we do to keep him away from the chickens?"

The warden opened his car door and shook his head. "Keep the trough full," he said, and pulled away.

For about a week the fox was there with the pigs, waiting for his dinner every day when Luanne returned home from work. The pigs never minded their visitor. Luanne stopped alongside the pen and watched, intrigued by the fox but marveling at the pigs even more. They were so gentle. They never bossed their dining companion around. And they were clean. She knew what everyone said about pigs, rolling in the mud, rooting around in the dirt. And it was true. But beyond that, they never messed up where they slept, and that was more than she could say for some animals. Most of all, it seemed to Luanne that pigs just wanted love. Whenever she neared the pen, Porkchop and Hambone abandoned whatever they were doing (usually eating) and waddled over to greet her, wagging their curly tails. She scratched their ears and told them how beautiful they were. They grinned back at her and oinked their appreciation and love right back.

One day the fox disappeared. The pigs seemed just as content without their dining companion. They were content, that is, until they decided to get out and explore the local epicurean offerings. Weighing nearly two hundred pounds each, they pretty much just walked through the enclosure whenever they wanted and took a leisurely stroll.

If there was any time to do any strolling of her own, Luanne hadn't found it. Every day was full of activity, with mornings starting abruptly. At times Corky awakened them, whining at the bottom of the loft ladder to be let out. Other times it was Vicky the white cat, scratching at the window. One day Luanne opened her eyes to the sound of a sharp *rat a tat tat* outside the window. "Look, Henry!" she said. It was a fat downy woodpecker, tufts of red on the sides of his head, perched on the metal ladder. His whole body bobbed as he pecked against the rung.

"You're not going to find your breakfast there," Luanne laughed. But the woodpecker kept trying.

She and Henry got up, backed down the ladder from the loft, went to the kitchen and opened the door to let Corky and the cats out. Henry started preparing breakfast and she went outside to open the chicken coop and collect the eggs. By the time she returned,

George was waiting by the kitchen door. The striped cat's purr was muffled by a sleek bullhead flopping in his mouth. Randy and his buddy had thrown a few of the catfish into the pond after a day of fishing in the stream down the road. The fish must have multiplied. This one was nearly as big as George, with brown scales and stubby whiskers on the sides of its face. George pawed at the fish's tail.

"Just take it away if you're going to do that." Luanne shooed George and his catch away. She understood that some animals were the hunters, while others were hunted, but it always made her sorry to witness the fact.

As she walked back into the house, the phone was ringing. She set down her basket of eggs and answered. "This is the dog control officer," the voice on the other end said. "Have you got a big dog?"

"Well," Luanne replied, "he's not that big but yeah, I guess."

"Your neighbor up the road is complaining of a big dog on their property, digging up their garden."

Luanne took a look around. She didn't see Corky in the house. He often loped around outside but rarely left the property, especially since the time he'd gone missing. She was surprised he'd wandered off. "I'll go get him," she said.

"I'm heading up there myself. If you don't pick up your dog, I'll have to take him to the pound."

Grumbling, Luanne grabbed a leash and headed through the field to the neighbor's. She wished they'd just called her, instead of the authorities. The closest neighbor was up the hill, around the bend, and beyond a grove of evergreens.

When she arrived, the dog control officer was already there talking to the neighbor, who stood with his hands on his hips. Corky was nowhere to be seen. Instead, Porkchop pushed his piggy nose into the dirt, enjoying grubs and crawly things in the well-kept garden.

Luanne knew at once it was her pig, but remained confused. "I thought you said my dog was here?"

"I didn't say *dog,*" the man growled. "I said *hog*. And what I need is for you to get your big fat hog out of here!"

"Oh, I will, I'm sorry," Luanne said, her cheeks burning. The leash she held was going to be useless. She tried calling and then pushing the pig, but that didn't work. "I'll be right back, I promise," she said.

"I don't want to have to come back here," the dog warden warned, but as he left he was chuckling. Luanne ran back to the house, found Hambone still in the pen beside the broken fence and hoped he'd stay put. She grabbed a loaf of Wonder bread to coax Porkchop away from the garden. When she returned to the neighbor's garden she apologized again and held out a slice of white bread. The portly pig accepted, and happily followed her home. Their walk was slow-going, but she smiled at her friend's little grunts and snorts, and scratched the top of his wiry-haired head. When they arrived back at the pen, Corky ran down from the house and joined her. "Let this be a lesson to you too," she said to him. "Don't go wandering off on me, ever." Corky jumped up and wrapped his paws around her waist.

Although she and Henry fixed the fence, the pigs got out again. "How are we going to keep them in?" Luanne asked.

Henry sighed. "I don't think we need to worry about that anymore."

Luanne stood silent.

The next week a truck pulled up the driveway. Henry talked to the driver for a while and shook his hand. Luanne stared down at the tire tracks in the mud. The driver laid down a ramp, while Henry opened the pen and tried to push the pigs out. Porkchop and Hambone would have no part of it. They looked up as if smiling and wagged their tails. Luanne swallowed hard. "This is how it must be," she told herself. "This is what you signed up for. Remember their names. You can't expect to have a farm and live off the land and not face this at some point." She squeezed her eyes tight to hold back the tears.

The two men pushed together; then they both pulled; then one pushed while the other pulled. Henry scratched his head. "How're we gonna get them in the truck?"

The driver reached into the truck cab. "I've got a way."

"Wait!" Luanne cried. She didn't know what he might produce, a rope, or a prod of some sort, but no way would her pigs last time on earth be spent pushed and frightened. She ran into the house and returned with the loaf of Wonder bread. "Here you go," she said, feeding a slice to Porkchop. She gave another slice to Hambone. "It's okay. Let's go now." She scratched Porkchop under the chin and walked slowly forward. The pigs followed. Henry and the driver quietly watched the slow-moving parade.

"Don't be afraid," she said. She placed a foot on the ramp and hesitated. The inside of the truck was dark and cold. "It's okay." Her voice wavered. She forced herself to take another step. Porkchop and Hambone followed her up into the truck. She threw her arms around their necks, hugged them, dropped the loaf of bread, and bolted out.

Henry shook the driver's hand again and the truck pulled away. Luanne ran over to the pond and sat on the big rock, her back to the pigpen. She couldn't hold back the tears any longer. "What have I done?" she cried. Her heart ached. She tried to push away the image of Porkchop following her trustingly, and Hambone wagging his spiral tail. "I'm sorry," she cried. "Forgive me."

She sat alone on the rock for some time before Corky came around to find her. He rested his head on her knee and she stroked his wiry hair until the sun began to set. "Thank you, old friend," she said. They walked back up to the house together.

On Saturday morning, Tom arrived at the door with a sharp ax, and Luanne knew it wasn't going to be a good day. Henry had decided it was time to take care of some of the chickens—about thirty of them. This was not a job a guy could easily do by himself, and Luanne knew that she would get pressed into service. But she refused to be anywhere near where the actual chopping was taking place.

So Henry and Tom went out back by the chicken coop, and Luanne set a big cast-iron pot in the pit near the side of the house and got a fire going. Just as the water started simmering, she heard a ruckus of clucks, then a loud squawk, and then the *thwack* of an ax. She startled at the noise.

Pretty soon Henry walked over and handed her a limp, dead chicken to de-feather.

Luanne took hold of the chicken by its legs. She always loved to watch the chickens peck about in the yard and chase a bug in the dirt. With so many chickens running about in the yard, she couldn't tell them all apart. Just the same, she let her eyes well up and blur so that there could be no way to determine which one she was holding.

With the water just below a boil, she dunked the chicken in to soften the quills, removed it, gave it a gentle shake, and began plucking. Wearing gloves just made the motion more difficult, so she rested the carcass on a towel on her lap and set to work with her bare hands. *God, thank you for this food you have provided for us*, she prayed as she worked as gently as possible. Every time she heard the squawk and the thwack, she jumped. She was grateful they'd have plenty of food for the winter, but she would never get used to the process.

After she'd plucked about six birds, she gathered them up, brought them into the kitchen and covered them with a cloth. When she returned outside, one of the cars was gone.

"Henry?" she called. "Tom?"

No answer. "Henry!" she called, louder. Her first thought was that they were rushing someone to the hospital with an ax wound but, no, they surely would have told her. They must have snuck away when she'd gone into the house. She stomped onto the porch, fuming that they'd abandoned the job half done. After more than an hour Tom's car pulled into the driveway and the two men stumbled out, a six-pack tucked under each arm. When they saw Luanne scowling and glaring, they tried to look innocent.

"Henry!" she snapped.

"Aw, give him a break. A guy needs some refreshment for all that work," Tom said. The men snickered and slunk back behind the house.

Tom was no help. A bad influence. But no, she couldn't blame it on Tom. The ax thwacked again, and the men finished the job. Henry came over and helped Luanne finish the plucking. She knew it was his way of saying he was sorry.

Chapter 10

Paperboy

THE HOUSE WAS still far from done. They needed walls. Only curtains separated the dining room and bedroom areas. "I have to wash my walls and hang them out to dry," Luanne told her friend at school.

That wasn't all. The floors had no flooring, the windows no casings, the porch no railings, the loft bedroom no real stairs. That was just the beginning. Outside, land needed to be graded, barns enlarged, wood chopped, fences built. The old school bus, no longer in working condition, was dismantled and hauled away, chunk by chunk. Luanne had felt her eyes well up as she'd watched the pickup truck drive off with the scraps of dented aqua metal. It had been home.

As soon as they fixed one problem, something else broke. Although they had two vehicles, one she drove to work and an older pickup truck for the farm, one was forever acting up. One morning Luanne walked out of the house to see Henry pushing the truck with the garden tractor.

"Henry. What on earth?" she asked. But truthfully, the sight didn't totally surprise her.

"Won't go into reverse," Henry answered. The way the house sat at the top of the hill, there was no room to drive the truck around in a circle. The dense woods at the back of the lot and the steep hill in the front left only a narrow level area for parking. Henry nudged the truck's rear fender forward, turning it around so that he could drive without having to back all the way down the long, twisting driveway.

Another day, the truck moaned and groaned when Henry turned the key. "Guess she needs a little push," he said. So out he went and started up the tractor.

"Is this a good idea?" Luanne called from the truck's front seat.

"Just keep the door open and hang on!" Henry pushed with the tractor until the truck started rolling forward.

Luanne reached over to steady the wheel and hit the brake so that Henry had time to turn off the tractor and climb in the truck before it rolled down the driveway.

One day Luanne's car wouldn't start. "I'll drop you off at work," Henry said. "I don't have any carpet cleaning to do today, so I can stop by the post office to pick up that package, too." The package contained several tool kits they'd ordered for family members for Christmas gifts. Luanne had spent so much time selecting just the right gift, and couldn't wait to get them home and wrap them up.

But Henry didn't arrive to pick her up after work. She called, but no answer. Finally she accepted a ride home. When she got out of the car at the end of the driveway, Henry was standing there talking to a tow truck driver.

"You said your truck was *kind of* in the pond," the tow truck driver protested. "This is *all the way* in the pond!"

157

Muddy tire tracks ran from up by the house, veering off the driveway and down the grassy hill. The front end of the truck was submerged in the 14-foot depth, and only a bit of the blue bed stuck out.

"How?" was all she could utter.

"I was nudging it with the tractor and...," Henry answered.

The tow truck guy scratched the side of his head. "I'll have to go get the big rig. This is more of a job than I thought. I'll be back." He turned and mumbled, "Wait till the guys in the shop hear this!"

As the too-small tow truck pulled off, Luanne and Henry stared at what was left of their own vehicle, protruding out of the pond.

"Think you ran over any fish?" Luanne asked at last.

Henry laughed a little, and then turned serious. "What if they can't get it out?" He paced near the muddy bank. "Hang on a second!" He hiked up the road to a woodpile and returned with a plank. He placed it on the ground from the bank to the truck bed.

"What are you doing?"

"Don't worry." Henry carefully shuffled across the plank and squatted down, feeling under the cold water. He held onto the side of the truck with his free hand.

"What are you doing?" Luanne repeated.

"Aha!" Henry pulled a soggy box out of the water and held it up over his head. "The tool kits!" he said with a boyish smile.

She couldn't stay mad.

The sun had set by the time the tow rig returned and pulled the truck out of the drink. "How much?" Henry asked the operator. "Can you bill us?"

The driver adjusted his cap. He looked up at the half-finished house and back at the pond. "I reckon I could take your truck in payment," he said. Water leaked out of the cracks in the doors. "For parts."

"You've got a deal." Henry pumped his hand.

Word spread around town pretty fast, and for a while every time they went into the general store someone would ask, "Hey Henry, have you washed your truck today?"

It wasn't a routine checkup. Henry's cold symptoms lingered and he felt rundown and dizzy. The doctor didn't like the blood work results. Or the MRI. They'd found a spot. "Pancreatic cancer," the doctor said.

Luanne sat in the Veteran's Hospital beside a young doctor with a smiley-face necktie peeking out of his lab coat. "This is not a well man," he said, scanning Henry's thick chart. "He's already been through a lot. His labs are elevated in so many areas, it's hard to find one that's good. He'll need surgery, but…" The doctor's voice trailed off. Luanne closed her eyes and tried to find a prayer. She knew there was a God, but she never truly believed that she deserved His blessings. Maybe he cared about Henry. Henry, who was sick and vulnerable, lying on his back in the hospital bed, covered by a thin beige blanket, monitors beeping.

After the surgery the doctor returned to the room, and this time not even his necktie was smiling. He scribbled a few notes and looked up. "Things went as well as expected, but I'll be honest. There's only about a 10 percent chance of survival beyond one or two years."

Luanne stared. The words were beyond her grasp. She and Henry had just started a life together. They were only beginning to build their farm. Her chin trembled, but even crying didn't seem real.

"And another thing." The doctor looked her in the eyes. "Pancreatic cancer is strongly tied to severe alcohol consumption. I'm talking four or more drinks a day."

Her stomach wrenched. All along she'd wondered. Worried. Denied. Suspected. Rationalized. She wanted to do the right thing, but best intentions weren't always enough.

RESPONSIBILITY

The goldfish wriggled in the plastic bag from the pet shop. Her husband complained that they already had enough wildlife, for Pete's sake, and she was wasting her time with such trifling pursuits. True she had a dog, a cat, and a cage of gerbils their three children adored. No telling why a goldfish pond became so important. She just longed for a piece of country, a way to surround herself with more animals.

So one day when the kids were at school and her husband was at work in his accounting office, she found a shovel in the shed and dug a small hole in the rock garden. She poured the cement mix she'd bought at the hardware store, adding cool water from the hose. Because she couldn't find a trowel, she rubbed the cement with her hands and then quickly washed them off before it dried. A few hours later she looked at the four fish, eyes bugging and little mouths puckering, and wondered how long they could survive in the bag. She touched the edge of the pond. It felt firm enough, so she filled the pond with water and released the goldfish. She beamed, watching them swim around free. She'd done a good thing, giving them a home where they would be loved and admired.

For the longest time she sat by the pond and smiled at what she'd created. A little Eden away from the harsh demands of trying to be a good wife. The fish swimming unconstrained made her feel free too.

When the kids came back from school, she took them to the pond to show them their new pets. "You can each name one," she said, planning to name the last one Angela. But when they looked down past the snapdragons, something was clearly amiss. The water was gray and milky. Two of the fish drifted slowly, sides heaving as if gasping for breath. The others floated upside down. A cloudy substance had accumulated around their gills. Luanne turned the kids around quickly and ushered them inside.

"What happened?" Randy had asked. She couldn't lie. The kids knew the fish were dead. But she couldn't tell them that it had been her fault. The cement hadn't been mixed properly or hadn't dried properly, and it had hardened in their gills. The poor things. All she wanted to do was to give them a beautiful home. She went back outside, fighting back tears, burying each soul under a snapdragon.

Weeks later, the empty pond seemed a shame. The cement had surely hardened by then. She'd learned her lesson and was ready to try again. Armed with a new little baggie from the pet shop, she knelt in the garden and very gently slid the goldfish into the water. Although their swooshing tails were really a means of propulsion, she took it to indicate that they were happy there. And at last everything seemed right.

The very next day, however, she startled a tiger-striped figure crouched in the garden. With her next step, the neighbor's cat scurried away, a fish hanging from its jaw. It was too late. All the goldfish had been devoured.

"I'm sorry," she'd sobbed beside the restless water. "I didn't mean it. I'm sorry." She'd meant well, but good intentions weren't enough. She'd destroyed precious life. She'd never forgive herself. The cement pond remained empty for as long as she lived there.

A few weeks after Henry came home from the hospital, his pal Tom came to visit. Luanne handed him a mug. "Not a little nip of something in here, is there?" he asked.

"No." She gave Henry a firm look and busied herself in the kitchen.

"Good you're up and about. But you had to go on disability, eh?" Tom took a swig of the steaming coffee.

"Yep. Sold all the carpet-cleaning machines to my old boss. It took more strength than I had to lug those around."

"You probably shouldn't be out chopping wood like I seen you, either." Tom said.

"Can't do as much as I wish I could."

Tom paused and set down the mug. "You going to be okay? I mean, without the income?"

"We'll get by," he said, brushing the question off.

"Plus," Luanne called from the kitchen, "Henry's got a paper route."

"Ha!" Tom let out a hearty laugh. "Henry, you're a paperboy now?"

"Yep," Henry returned. "Rural delivery, car route. They drop off the papers at the general store and I just drive around and take them to the houses."

"Paperboy," Tom laughed. "Well, I'll be hanged. Do ya like it?"

"Guess so. It's pretty early in the morning, though. Before the chickens are up."

"That is early. Well, if you have my house, don't be late. I like to read *The Old Farmer's Almanac* column with my coffee."

Every day Henry got up to deliver the papers, and once a week he received an envelope with payment tucked in the top of the stack of newspapers. Inside the envelope someone added a mini booklet, a few inches tall, all of four pages. One time Luanne noticed one of the tiny fliers on the table. "What's this?"

"I dunno, there's one in the papers, every week," Henry said.

She held it up and read. *How do you get to heaven?* The booklet contained some information and the address of a church in Waterville. Luanne believed in heaven, and she assumed that if you were good enough, you'd get there. But just how good did you have to be? Doubt crept into her mind. Furthermore, according to the booklet, it wasn't all about being good. It was about accepting a gift, whether she deserved it or not. How could that be? Her own father had found little use for her. Would her heavenly Father really give her a gift?

She found another tiny booklet under some papers. "Finding Love, Joy, and Peace." Again, the address of the church. For the first time, she longed to know more. "I think we should go," she told Henry. "Why don't we try it out?"

"I don't know," he replied. "Too busy."

He changed his mind a few weeks later. They were driving along the road and it had been sprinkling. Then the sun came out and lit up the sky. As they started down a steep hill, a magnificent rainbow arched right in front of them. The soft colors radiated with a robust glow. Luanne didn't dare move in the car's seat—even one breath might make the beauty disappear. One side of the rainbow started beyond the top of the hill. And the other seemed to end just above a church. A white clapboard church. The church in Waterville.

Henry pulled to a stop in the middle of the road.

"Well," Luanne gasped. "What do you think now?"

"Can't argue with that," he said.

They visited the church that very Sunday. As they walked in the door, an older woman greeted them and asked for their names. When Henry told her, she squealed. "Oh! You're our paperboy!" She shook his hand and beamed. The small congregation, about thirty people on a good day, surrounded them. They were farmers and workers and teachers, moms and sons and daughters. Luanne felt right at home in the pew.

The pastor spoke about loving thy neighbor. She looked around at the congregation wondering who her neighbor was. Was it the old woman with the cane? The little boy holding his daddy's hand? The young couple cradling a baby? She'd been in other churches before, but this was the first time it felt personal, like there was a reason she was there. Henry put his arm around her shoulder. When the final hymn rang out in clanky piano and voices both beautiful and shrill, Luanne sang too. "Love lifted me, love lifted me. When nothing else could help, love lifted me."

She went to bed that night encouraged by the warmth of the service. The next morning she was awakened early by a noise. It was still dark out. She climbed down from the loft to investigate. Henry was returning home from his paper route. He didn't usually awaken her when he made his way in the house and back up to bed, but he'd knocked into the frying pan on the counter and it had clattered into the sink.

"What's wrong?" Luanne asked, peering into the dark.

Henry dropped into his chair. "I saw a moose. A big one, with huge antlers, in the middle of the road!"

Luanne sat down on the couch and listened.

"It was dark, but I could still see. It was so huge! And I could see its breath, and it snorted."

"Wow!"

"It wouldn't move. So I just backed up and came home."

"Did you get your papers delivered?" she asked.

"No," he said wearily. "I'll do it later."

She got up and bent over to give him a kiss. That's when she smelled it. She wanted to walk away, to pretend she hadn't noticed. Maybe then it didn't really exist. She wanted to go upstairs to the loft and go back to sleep. But she couldn't. She knew before she even asked. "Henry have you ... been drinking? Already?"

Henry leaned back and closed his eyes. "There was a moose in the road."

Chapter 11

The Little Lamb

THE EWE PACED uncomfortably. Luanne spread fresh hay in the stall and rubbed the pregnant sheep's side. The ewe panted.

Lambing season was both Luanne's favorite and most stressful time of year. She was on a cloud, lightheaded and awed, watching a new life come into the world. She ached to her very depth, however, when something went wrong. A week earlier, a ewe had been in labor for hours too long. Luanne sat with her, comforting her, encouraging her, while the ewe looked back at her, eyes wild with fear. She longed to do something to take that terror away. When at last the water broke and the lamb began to emerge, Luanne cheered. But then progress stopped.

"I can't get away from the office," the vet had said. "You'd better bring her in here to me, and fast!"

Luanne's heart raced. How were they ever going to get a huge, heavy, uncomfortable, struggling sheep in labor into the truck? As she bent over to wrap a blanket around the ewe, Arthur the ram bleated and gave her a swift kick in the rear. Luanne stumbled to the ground. "We're not hurting her, Arthur," she promised.

Together, she and Henry made a sling and lifted the ewe into the back of the truck. "I'm riding with her. I don't want her to be alone." Luanne huddled beside her while Henry sped to the doctor's office.

They traveled over the bumpy dirt road. When they reached the railroad tracks, Luanne pounded on the cab window. Henry turned around to look. Luanne was grinning and giving him the thumbs up. A baby lamb had been born.

Hopefully, this birth would go easier. The ewe was an experienced mother, and a good one. Luanne stroked her side. "You're a good gal. You can do this," she said. She left her alone, promising to check back later.

After dinner, she and Henry raced back to the barn. Inside, everything was still. Luanne's breath hung expectantly in the air. She stood on her tiptoes and peeked over the side of the stall. There, nestled in the matted hay, were two tiny white balls of wool.

"Twins!" Henry said, adjusting a heat lamp to keep them nice and warm.

"We did it!" Luanne clasped her hands together and closed her eyes for a moment. She couldn't help but praise God when witnessing this miracle. How could she not feel blessed by His marvelous creations? She gazed happily at the new family.

"Are you crying?" Henry laughed gently.

"No," she denied, wiping away a tear.

The ewe had cleaned the babies and was nudging one to stand and nurse. Luanne watched, scarcely breathing, as the baby awkwardly rose on long, skinny limbs to take its first wobbly steps. The lamb nursed, woolly tail moving round and round in a blissful circle. The mama bleated gently to her baby.

At first everything seemed fine. But the ewe only tended to one twin. The other curled up in the hay, motionless. She blinked her tiny eyes weakly.

"Feed your baby," Luanne urged.

The ewe pushed it aside.

Luanne had heard of this happening. Sometimes the mother rejected the weaker twin. The baby's legs were limp; she was unable to stand on her own. Luanne lifted the lamb ever so gently and held her up to the mother, but she was too frail to suck. If this lamb was to survive, it was all up to her and Henry.

"Get her inside and keep her warm," Henry said. "I'll get some milk from the mother."

Luanne wrapped the lamb in a warm blanket and snuggled her in her lap by the fire. When Henry returned, she used an eyedropper to drip some of the mother's milk into the lamb's mouth. The milk ran right back out. Luanne kept trying. "Drink, sweet Lorrie," she said, calling the lamb by her favorite girl's name. No matter what, if something happened, the little lamb would not die an anonymous creature.

All night long she worked over Lorrie, offering drops of milk, coaxing her to drink. Her eyes grew heavy but Luanne forced herself to stay awake. Lorrie needed her. She prayed simply and earnestly, *God, please, let this little sweet creature of yours live.*

When at last Luanne did drift off to sleep, she awoke with a start. She looked down at the lamb pressed against her chest, so still. She placed her shaking hand on the lamb's side. She was breathing! Lorrie had made it through the night!

Despite the milestone, the lamb still lay so still, too weak to raise her head. Luanne didn't dare leave her, dripping milk from the eyedropper into her mouth every half hour. She cuddled the lamb in her arms, making up for the love and warmth Lorrie was missing from her mama. She spoke softly, telling her she was good and wanted and beautiful. Lorrie looked up at her with utter trust. Luanne felt blessed by the awesome responsibility to be the provider of such care. She would do anything for the little life, if only she would survive.

The next day Lorrie responded a little more. She lifted her head. She pushed her nose against Luanne's shoulder. Luanne made a sling to hold her up and practice bearing weight on her wobbly legs.

That night Luanne curled with Lorrie on the recliner chair. Knowing she needed more than what an eyedropper could give, Luanne touched a baby bottle to the lamb's mouth. "Just a little," she cooed. "Take just a little bit, Lorrie." She wrapped her arms around the lamb so she could feel her warmth.

As exhaustion overtook her, she rocked the lamb in her arms. "Please, God," she prayed over and over, "save this little lamb. She's your creature, and she's so weak and helpless. She needs you so much." She never realized there was a deeper meaning to her prayers.

Luanne had just drifted off when a sudden thought startled her awake. *Take this lamb to church tomorrow.* It was not just an idle thought, but the feeling jolted her, strong and persistent.

What? The very idea was ridiculous. How could she bring an animal into church? It was crazy! Why would she ever do such a thing? What would she say? She was no good at speaking in front of people. The next morning, however, the feeling wouldn't go away.

As she got dressed for church, she looked at precious Lorrie sleeping in her snug little box. So fragile, yet there she was, enduring. Maybe she would inspire others. Before she could change her mind, Luanne wrapped the lamb in a soft, blue blanket and headed for the door.

"Uh, wait." Henry looked at her in disbelief. "What are you doing?"

"I'm taking Lorrie to church," she said.

"You've got to be kidding!"

But now that she'd finally decided, she was sure. Nothing was going to stop her. Henry just shrugged and went along with it. They piled into the truck and bumped down the dirt road to church.

Luanne paused outside the white clapboard building and took a breath. "No turning back now," she thought. They walked up the steps where the pastor greeted people as they entered. "Good morning, Pastor Tom," she said. Trying to hide Lorrie behind the blue blanket, she asked if she might say a few words after the service. The lamb did not escape his gaze, but the pastor just raised his eyebrows and nodded.

Luanne, Henry, and Lorrie sat near the back of the church. Lorrie didn't utter a sound and slept contentedly. When the service was nearly over, Luanne was invited to the front. She thought she would fall down from trembling as she walked forward. A hot flush stung her cheeks. When she unwrapped the blanket, a collective gasp rose from the congregation. *Oh no, what have I done?* she worried.

The worshippers grew silent as Luanne explained how she had stayed up night after night, feeding the lamb, cuddling her and praying for her. She explained how the helpless little being needed her, depended on her. Then she set Lorrie down on the altar. The little hooves clicked on the polished wood. Luanne steadied her as she stood with wobbly limbs. With all her might, Lorrie struggled to stand.

Then the words flowed out. "*I* am like this lamb," Luanne realized. "I am weak, and I need help to stand on my own. I cannot do it alone. But I don't have to stand alone. I am blessed because I have the Lord." Without hesitation, she recited the words to the Psalms, words that she didn't even realize she knew. "The Lord is my shepherd, I shall not want ..."

When she was done, she didn't dare look up. How had her message been received? Did she look like a fool, bringing a lamb to church? Would she ever be able to show her face in church again? All she could do was pick up Lorrie and make a dash for the door. As she tried to hustle down the aisle, however, a little girl in the front row jumped up to pat Lorrie. A man with a hearing aid reached out to touch her as they passed. A young couple put their baby's hand on Lorrie's soft fleece. At the end of the aisle, a woman hugged Lorrie and then hugged Luanne, too.

As she sat down, she felt as if arms were still embracing her. That was when she realized, when she was praying for Lorrie every night, she was also praying for herself. As difficult a struggle life was and would prove to be, she did not have to do it alone. For as much as she loved the little lamb, she realized, she was loved, too.

Chapter 12

Sugaring Off

MARCH WAS NOT quite spring in terms of the snow that still lay a foot deep on the hillside and the chill that required her to bundle up in a turtleneck, sweatshirt and heavy coat just to go outside and feed the chickens. But it was spring in terms of maple trees, and the sap was running.

Luanne peeked into a metal pail hanging on a tree. She dipped her finger in and tasted the liquid, clear as water. A smile spread across her lips. "Sweet!" She let some sap drip down for Corky.

"We've got a lot more." Henry eagerly lifted the bucket and emptied it into a large metal milk can on the toboggan.

The day Henry came home with a truckload of pails and spouts he'd traded for a slab of fresh bacon, Luanne felt happier than a bumblebee in a field of clover. Maple sugaring! Just the thought of it put her closer to her Vermont ancestors. This was just what they needed. They had maple trees up in the woods behind the house, and they even had permission to tap a few trees on their friend's property down the road, ready to produce amazing sap just for them. The March weather was perfect—cold nights and warm spring days.

They'd wasted no time in drilling holes into the trees, about two inches deep. Henry drilled at a slight upward angle so the sap would pour out easily. Then they'd pounded in the spouts and hung the buckets. Luanne had gasped as the first drops of sap hit the bottom of the pails. A secret, concealed within each tree, now flowed as a blessing of sweet sustenance.

"I think we've got enough," Henry said that morning, "to start firing."

Of course they had no sugarhouse, but that didn't stop them. There was an old stove in the basement and, since it wasn't being used for anything else, it became their site for sugaring off.

They pulled the sled, heavy with the full milk can, right up to the basement door and hefted it inside. Topper and Chief followed eagerly. Henry rigged up his own evaporator, a cooler on a stool on top of a table, with the spigot positioned so that it dripped into a large pan atop the stove.

"Okay, enough," Luanne said, raising her hand. "Don't put in too much or it will boil over." They watched as the sap simmered and began to bubble.

"It's awful steamy in here," Luanne said, rolling up her sleeves. As the gallons of sap boiled down, moisture escaped into the room. An ordinary sugarhouse would have a tall chimney pipe to vent the steam out, but their makeshift room had no such provision.

"Yeah, but we'd better not leave. This sap can boil away quickly and burn," Henry added.

The more the sap cooked, the steamier it got in the basement. The moistness stuck thick on their skin. Who knew maple sugaring could be so messy? Although it was a sweet mess.

After three hours, the last of the sap was on the fire. Henry's face blazed red as a rooster's wattle. He stripped down to his undershirt, which was soaked with sweat. His hair stuck to his head.

Luanne's boots made a sucking sound as she walked on the sticky floor. She nearly wilted in the humidity. Cracking the windows and door did little to help. "At last, looks like we're nearly done. How many buckets of sap did we use?"

"Near all. Forty."

She peered into the pan on the stove. "And ...that's all?" She knew the sap would boil down, but after weeks of collecting and hauling, and all day boiling, she expected forty gallons of sap to make more than the meager amount at the bottom of the pan.

"Yup," said Henry, beaming through the sweat and grime. "About a gallon here. A gallon of Vermont maple syrup!"

Empty sap buckets littered the floor. Pots, pans, spoons, and utensils were scattered everywhere. The windows fogged over and the walls glistened with beads of tacky steam. But there it was, on the stove. Dark amber-colored syrup, thick and pure and beautiful. "We did it!" she said, hugging Henry.

"We did it," he said. "We did it!"

"And look!" Luanne pointed out the streaked window, where fat white flakes pattered down. Even though they were both dripping and sticky and exhausted, they ran outside and caught the snow in a shallow bowl, and when the bowl was filled, they drizzled the warm syrup on top. Hitting the cold snow, the syrup hardened to a firm, chewy candy. They pulled the candy off and gobbled the delicious sugar-on-snow, made with their very own sap from their very own farm by their very own hands.

The only thing sweeter than maple syrup was the arrival of spring babies. When the weather warmed, Luanne and Henry checked for ducklings down by the pond. They spotted a solitary gray duck egg in a nest in the tall grass. The mother duck would never have left it unattended. Luanne frowned. "I don't think she's coming back." She ran her finger along the soft, cold shell. "We could rig up a box and a heat lamp and try to hatch it," she suggested.

"Hmm. Not that easy." Henry touched the egg. "You have to keep the temperature even, and I don't know how we'd do that with our old, rickety heat lamp. We'd need to keep some humidity in there. And then, there's turning the egg ... how many times? Five or six. Seven?"

"Maybe we can slip the egg into another nest?" Luanne looked around. One brood of ducklings had just hatched. Luanne smiled as she watched the mama and fuzzy babies paddle in a wobbly row close to the shoreline. The happy little family. But no other eggs. "What about...The goose has a nest?" She brightened. "It worked for Mighty Duck!"

Earlier that month, a farmer across town asked if they'd take in a few of his fowl, stating that he was downsizing. He arrived with six chickens and an unlikely pair—a doting mother goose and a baby duck. "She hatched out that little duckling," he explained. "All her own eggs got taken by raccoons. You never heard such commotion, louder than a harvest thunderstorm. She flapped her wings and bellowed so pitifully. Well, I couldn't bear to

186

hear her cries. And the mama duck had so many eggs. ..."

Maybe he'd messed with the order of things a bit, but it seemed to work for the goose and the baby duck. From the moment they set webbed foot on the new farm, the duck followed around after Mama Goose. She stretched out her little short neck, trying to imitate the goose's long neck. Luanne took to calling her Mighty Duck, due to the way she strutted around with her chest puffed out, racing after the goose.

Luanne and Henry gently placed the abandoned duck egg in the goose's nest and hoped for the best. Sadly, that egg never hatched, but the goose did produce her own beautiful brood of three healthy goslings. The chicks wore feathers of the softest buff color, with darker gray on top. They had little bright eyes and tiny, pointy beaks. After only a week, the geese took their babies outside to hunt for bugs in the spring grass. No sight was sweeter than the awkward babies scurrying in a line. Every night, Luanne checked the corner of the barn, counted the three little geese to make sure they were all back safely inside and whispered good-night.

One afternoon the sky darkened and a torrential rainstorm burst from the skies. The drops pelted angrily against the windows.

Henry dashed outside to check that the sheep and goats had gone to shelter.

"I'm going to make sure everything's okay in the barn," Luanne said. She pulled on a coat and flipped up the hood. Hugging her arms across her chest, she scurried into the driving rain.

Little specks of white like melting snow caught her eye. Was it a freak hailstorm? She was about to run past to get to the barn but took a second look. It was like soft clumps of soaked cotton. Her heart sunk. The goslings!

The goose and gander must have hurried on ahead, assuming their babies were right behind. But in the sudden downpour, the little ones hadn't been able to keep up. She stifled a whimper and knelt down in the puddle. *Please let them be alive.* Luanne quickly scooped the goslings into her arms and rushed back to the house.

Henry met her inside. "Oh no!" He rushed to hand her a bath towel and she wrapped the babies gently. They didn't move. The wet goslings looked like shriveled white peaches, their feathers not yet fully in. Their heads hung limply to the side.

"We have to do something!" Luanne ran to the bathroom and returned with the hair dryer. Quickly she plugged it in and blew it over the near-drowned geese. The soft feathers started to fluff.

"Keep it up," Henry said.

She held the dryer over them ever so gently. Two of the geese stirred, raising their heads and opening their eyes.

"They're alive!" Luanne cried. "But..." She continued working over the third goose. It still didn't move.

Henry cupped the dried goslings in his hand. "I'd better get these two back with their mama. That's the best place for them. I'll ... take care of the other one after."

No, Luanne thought as Henry turned. *No one would be "taking care" of this gosling. It was going to survive.* She rocked as she held the little bird, pressing it close to her chest.

She would not lose this beautiful creature. "I won't give up on you," she whispered.

With her pinky, she gently rubbed the gosling's chest in light little circles. She moved its tiny legs. Anything, she thought, to get the circulation going. When she put her finger gently back on its chest again, she thought she felt some life. She caught her breath. It was just on the verge. If she gave up, it would be gone. *I have to keep going.* Without hesitation, she bent over and blew gently into the gosling's tiny beak. She rubbed its chest some more. "Come on," she said, "breathe."

Henry came back inside, bringing a burst of cold air with him, and quickly put some more logs in the stove and stoked the fire. He huddled next to Luanne to keep the warmth close. "Don't give up," he said softly.

The next time Luanne blew air in the little beak, she felt a tiny bit of motion. She cupped her hands around the baby bird and held it close to her neck. Henry put his arm around her, and they enveloped the gosling.

"It's alive," she whispered, tears welling in her eyes.

They placed the baby in a box by the fire, wrapped up in the towel.

"Do you realize you just gave CPR to a goose?" Henry asked.

The little bird tucked his tiny legs up under himself and seemed to heave a sigh. It was a miracle. All three goslings were saved.

Corky had been out in the rain, too, and had rushed inside and curled up on his blanket by the loft stairs, his nose tucked in tight. Luanne crouched beside him and scratched his gray chin. Very gently. He let out a deep sigh like an old man. She struggled to come up with how old he was. He was already middle-aged when they moved up to the farm. She remembered him playing with Randy, chasing each other around the house in the city when Randy had been a young boy. Corky had to be twelve or thirteen. He'd been by her side through so much. "My faithful friend," she said, kissing the tip of his nose. Over the next weeks she spent as much time with him as she could, resting beside him, telling him how loved he was. And when his time came, it was gentle and peaceful. She cried. She'd miss her friend. "Forgive me," she said, kneeling by a rock in the field where he was buried, "for not having the power to keep you here with me forever."

When Luanne walked into the classroom at work, Barbara was sitting alone at her desk. Her face was pale and she held a tissue to her eyes.

"Everything okay?" Luanne asked. She crouched beside the younger woman.

Barbara wiped her eyes and tried to smile, but admitted shakily, "I feel awful."

"Are you ill? Let me take you to the nurse."

"No, no. I'm okay. It's just," her voice grew soft, "my dog...my dog died last night."

Luanne felt a pang in her heart too. It was always painful to lose a pet. "Oh, I'm so sorry. What happened?"

Barbara brushed a damp strand of hair from her cheek. "I had her tied out in the shed. I don't like to, but you know Betsy, apt to wander off after something or another, and we'd seen a coyote around. She'd just had a litter of pups, did I tell you that? So many! Thirteen of the sweetest little things, black and brown, Cute as a bug's ear."

"That's a lot of puppies! What happened last night?" Luanne asked.

"Last night," Barbara's lip quivered. "Did you hear that thunderstorm come rolling in? I'm telling you, some of those claps scared the daylights out of me. I'm sure they terrified Betsy. But I couldn't go out and check on her till the rain let up. I just expected she'd be there, nursing her babies, minding her young. But when I got there, the pups were all alone, whimpering. And right behind them, broken glass. Their poor mama must have been so afraid of the thunder, she jumped through the window. I ran over, but it was too late. The rope was too short." She looked down at her feet. "Betsy was hanged."

Luanne gasped. "Oh, the poor thing! I'm so, so sorry. That must have been horrible."

"She was so young. So young to have puppies. I feel awful. I was the one who tied her up."

"Don't think that," Luanne said. "You did your best. Do you need any help?"

"Well," she sniffed, "Betsy's buried down by the old willow. But the pups … they're barely six weeks old. I was up all night trying to feed them. But thirteen! Do you, maybe, know anyone …?"

Luanne nodded. She'd been wanting a dog since they'd lost Corky. "I'll be there after school," she said.

That afternoon, Luanne knelt before a wriggling pack of dark fur nestled together in a box on the porch. Mostly Labradors, with a little hound mixed in, and round little bellies. If only she could become a puppy and crawl in the box and snuggle among them! They let up a racket of whimpers.

"You miss your mama, don't you?" Luanne picked up one and then another, cradling their tiny bodies close to hers, drawing in their sweet puppy breath. Others tumbled around her knees. "It's okay," she crooned. "You'll be okay."

"Seems like all they do is eat. If you take one, it'll need extra feedings," her co-worker said.

"I can do that."

"I'm keeping this one," Barbara said, reaching for a chubby girl pup, the only brown one in the litter. "Most like Betsy. I found homes for several others. If you took one, that would be wonderful. They need a good home. Which one do you want?"

Luanne looked at the sleepy pup licking her arm. Mostly black, with white on his chest and a white tip on his quivering tail. He was smaller and quieter than his brothers and sisters. "I'll take this one," she said, stroking his neck. She placed him back down on the ground while she made the arrangements. When she turned back around, another little black pup was curled up against the first. They looked up at her with hope in their eyes.

When she returned home and walked into the kitchen, Henry was there making a pot of vegetable soup for dinner. She showed him the puppy nuzzled against her neck.

"Why, hello little guy!" Henry ruffled the dog's ears.

"What do you think of Topper for a name?" Luanne asked.

"That's good," Henry answered.

"And what do you think we should name this one?" She pulled the other puppy out from under her coat.

Henry smiled.

"I couldn't just leave him there without his best friend, could I?"

"No," said Henry, accepting both dogs into his arms. "I suppose you couldn't."

DEVOTION

A family friend had found a stray hound in the woods. Luanne offered a trade: a stack of firewood for the dog. Her husband might not be happy about the addition, but her three young kids would be over the moon!

Most would say it was a fair trade. After all, to most observers, he wasn't really much of a dog. His face was young and round but his skin hung in baggy wrinkles, defined ribs circling his frame like the hoops of a barrel. His broad skull featured sad, drooping ears. If you could call them ears. One contained ragged bite marks around the edge; the other appeared Velcroed to his neck with thistles and burrs. His coat revealed some shade of brown or black, unless that was just dirt.

The tall man stood behind the dog, hands clasped as if apologizing for this baggage on the suburban house's narrow doorstep. "No collar. Starving. Probably abused." The man shook his head. "Looks like he's been in the woods for a long time. We couldn't just leave him there. Knowing how you like dogs and all, Lu … well, we didn't know what else to do."

There was nothing obviously becoming about the half-starved sack of bones. But Luanne knew better. "He's beautiful," she said. The dog looked up at her with eyes that consumed his face, deep and liquid with midnight black centers.

Every dog has eyes that make you want to smile, laugh, or even cry. But these eyes were different. You know the look of an old man who's lived a life of hardships and poverty, been beaten down and ready to give up? It was that kind of look, only these eyes showed no bitterness or resentment. Deep down, they embodied a soft flickering glow that reflected—could it be?—all was good.

Luanne bent down and stroked the dog's back, shuddering as she felt his spine, as if each protrusion hurt her as well. The day was colder than the frost in a pumpkin patch, but Luanne removed her heavy coat and wrapped it around the shivering hound. "You did the right thing."

Her husband poked his head out the kitchen door. "He's filthy."

Luanne let the comment pass. Only she saw the truth. Her husband glimpsed a grubby mutt. Her friend viewed a hopeless stray. But Luanne saw love.

"You know, you really didn't have to give me anything in return," the man said, backing down the steps. "He's just an ol' stray anyway." He shook his head. "But thanks for the firewood!"

The trade was intentional. To Luanne, the dog had value and therefore earned something of value in exchange. The man left, slamming his station wagon gate tight against his payment of logs.

A few days later a neighbor friend visited, remarking that her kids mentioned seeing a beautiful dog next door. She took one look at the emaciated hound scratching its ears and raised her eyebrows. "Beautiful?"

Luanne blushed, thinking of her own five-foot-nothing stature and her figure that tended to fill out around the middle. She moved her hand protectively to the dog's back and nodded. Maybe if she'd felt beautiful herself, she would never have related to the small and the homely. "He's beautiful to me!"

She brought the dog into the house. He sat still, waiting for permission to budge. Luanne's three kids gathered around, excited about their new playmate. "Be gentle," Luanne said as the baby, Randy, tugged the dog's tail. The dog turned and licked Randy's face.

Luanne set down a bowl of food. The dog waited and watched, as if wondering if it was safe. He crept forward, his brown ears dragging on the floor, and then wolfed down huge gulps. He looked up ever so tentatively, his tail barely tapping on the linoleum.

Even when he seemed afraid, cowering under the table or in a corner, his tail tapped. Curled up among the soft blankets she'd laid on the floor, all tight and tucked in as if making himself into some sort of armor, the tiniest tip of his tail would start to wag when she walked by. And when surrounded by the kids, each one on the floor patting his head and shoulders and back, his tail spun with such a fury that it set everyone to giggling and rolling around. Luanne wondered if the little dog had ever had a family before—kids who loved him and played with him and maybe even were missing him now.

"What's his name?" her neighbor had asked.

"Happy," Luanne had replied instantly. Because, even though he'd been through hard times, was abandoned, starving, and likely mistreated, that was all she could see. Happy.

The dog already made her happy. A home wasn't complete without pets. Happy filled that empty place in her heart.

There was only one circumstance when Happy wasn't happy: whenever he saw a man. He hid when a male visitor came to the door. He ran off, tail between his legs, when the letter carrier approached. At first, he even shrank from her husband, who, in truth, liked animals, just not in the same way as Luanne. He felt pets were there to serve, to guard the house or chase mice. They should have a purpose. Growing up, he'd never owned a pet. When he met Luanne, he probably didn't know how much their feelings on animals differed. Of course, that was just one of their many differences.

Otherwise, Happy adored his new home, and Luanne imagined it far better than the sticks and leaves the stray must have slept on in the woods, or whatever else he'd endured. Maybe he'd been hit or kicked or even worse—and by the way he reacted, probably by a man. She figured that he'd been alone for months. The pads of his paws were worn, suggesting that he'd walked for miles. Maybe this was the first positive place he'd experienced in a long time.

Luanne studied his twitching front paw as he slept. What had it been like for Happy before now? Where had he lived and how had he become separated from his home? Was he lost? Or—Luanne swallowed hard—had someone carelessly tossed him away? Did he give his trust to someone who had turned around and rejected him? Or had he never had a chance at all, never been loved?

"I promise, I'll take good care of you," she whispered. They walked together early in the evenings when the streetlights came on, the kids were asleep, and her husband was engrossed in his classical music. They passed neighbors' houses with the lights shining from the windows, and she wondered what was going on inside. Were they warm? Comfortable? Did the wives sit on the sofa with their husbands after dinner, contentedly watching a TV program together? She had tried to appreciate the TV shows her husband enjoyed, but documentaries and news shows didn't interest her. She didn't care for those serious men droning on about complicated issues. Probably shows like *Meet the Press* really were over her head. As her husband frequently reminded her, she wasn't as well-educated as he was.

But walking with Happy, that she enjoyed. The breeze rustling through the evergreens, the moon peeking out from behind a branch, all centered her in the feeling that God was up there looking out for her. The same God who made the trees and the skies. That was a peaceful feeling.

They stayed outside until the moon was high. Happy remained by her side, glancing at her with adoring eyes. If she wasn't smart enough or cultured enough, the hound dog didn't care. She was who he wanted to be with. Happy's capacity to love amazed her. After being abandoned or abused or however he may have been mistreated, he didn't resent humans. He had every reason to distrust humans, yet he opened his heart to love again. With all her heart, Luanne wanted to be free of any resentment that impeded the love she had to give. If Happy could forgive, maybe, just maybe, she could too. Forgive her mother for leaving her, her father for neglecting her, her husband for demeaning her. Forgive anyone who had ever hurt her.

Chapter 13

The Truth

LUANNE WATCHED THE sun peek over the hills. At this hour, Henry was usually home from his paper route. She started a pot of coffee and sat down to wait. Maybe he'd been in an accident. What if he'd really hit a moose this time?

After another half hour she knew something was wrong. She peered out the window, called Tom and apologized for waking him.

"H'aint seen him," Tom said, "But my paper's not here."

She fought to keep her breathing from running away with her. Her hands trembled as she pulled on her coat, jumped in her car and rumbled down the driveway. She knew the route he drove. Maybe he was just stuck in the mud or had run out of gas.

There was no sign of him on the mountain road. She slowed the car. How much farther? At the next turn, something caught her eye. Tire tracks veering off the dirt road. Tall grasses and weeds flattened. Bushes parted. Henry used an old, blue Volkswagen for delivering papers. There, in the bushes, was a flash of blue metal. His car was swallowed in the overgrowth.

"Henry!" she pulled over and jumped out of the car. "Henry, are you okay?" The loose dirt gave way as she slid down the ditch to the car. It was tipped on its side, two wheels slightly off the ground. The front end was crumpled, the headlight smashed. She reached up and jerked open the passenger door. He was reclined in the driver's seat, head back, eyes closed.

"Henry!" At first glance, he didn't appear to be hurt. There was no blood, not even a scratch on his body. Crawling inside, she shook his shoulder. He turned his head and let out a deep noise. It wasn't a groan of pain, she realized. It was a snore. She looked down, and recoiled. *Oh, please, no!* Empty beer cans scattered about his feet.

Luanne shifted uncomfortably. "Thank you for taking us, Doctor."

Henry sat beside her, a pile of papers on the desk in front of them.

"How much?" the doctor asked him. "How much are you drinking?"

Luanne looked to Henry to answer, but he wouldn't meet her gaze.

"It's not …," Luanne started.

The doctor held up his hand and repeated. "How much a day?"

"Two six-packs." Henry replied.

Luanne shook her head. It couldn't be. Henry drank, but she'd never seen him stumbling, slurring. He just settled down and fell asleep. How could it be that bad?

But the doctor kept staring at Henry. "And?"

"And," Henry replied, "a fifth of whiskey."

Luanne's world fell apart.

That day Henry voluntarily submitted to a thirty-day rehab. Luanne hated leaving him there, hated accepting that he had a problem, hated admitting that she'd ignored the signs. She drove back to the farm, parked the car, and sat in the driver's seat, numb. She'd had a long ride to think, but it did her no good. In the fading light of dusk, her surroundings took on a suspicious aura. The countryside she knew as beautiful instead appeared eerie. For the hundredth time she looked out over the land and thought maybe it really was too much. Maybe everything was wrong—the land, the animals, the house. They weren't equipped. They weren't enough. Henry wasn't perfect, by any means, but he was her husband and she loved him. She'd never wanted to do all this by herself. Tears trickled down her cheeks and soon she could hold back the sobs no longer. "I am all alone," she cried. "I am so alone."

Eventually, she had no more tears to cry. Nothing but darkness surrounded her. Not even a star twinkled in the sky. No lights shone from the house. The night was so still, the car door startled her as she got out and banged it closed. She dragged herself up to the steps and paused. Her faithful friend Corky wouldn't be there to greet her. When she opened the door she was met, instead, by two rambunctious Labradors, tumbling all over each other, yapping and nipping at her feet. They'd emptied every wastebasket in the house, unwound a roll of toilet paper, and strewn shredded magazine pages across every inch of the floor. She let them outside—she didn't have the heart to scold them. Sinking to her knees, she grabbed a trash can and began cleaning up the mess. If only she could clean up the rest of her problems as easily.

Later that night, too exhausted to even climb the ladder to the loft, she curled up in the recliner and slept fitfully.

In the morning she awoke to a weight on her stomach. Her eyes focused to discover Vicky's face peering into hers. Topper and Chief wrestled in the kitchen. Outside, the rooster crowed. Goats down in the pasture bleated. A duck called to its mate. Little by little, sounds of life crept through the window, rippling, growing, resounding. The farm she loved called out to her. There was work to be done, and it wasn't going to wait for Henry to get home and help. She got up, stretched, and opened the door for the cats and dogs. Warm air greeted her. "Okay, okay, I'm coming!" she called to the sheep up on the hill. She left her coffee mug empty on the counter; she'd get to that later. The animals must be hungry.

First the chickens. She opened up their door and they spilled out, clucking and pecking the ground. She scattered corn and then gathered the eggs, but she was rushing so much she dropped the whole basketful. After she tended to all the animals up near the house, she looked down toward the lower pasture and took a deep breath. Herkimer.

Herkimer was a young, endearing, black-and-white male calf when he first arrived, but now he was a bull. Luanne cautiously noted the horns starting to form. Whenever he saw her coming he'd put his head down and start running toward her. So, while the bovine duties had mainly fallen to Henry, now she had no choice.

She grabbed a rake, filled a pail with grain and walked down the pasture. Topper and

Chief trotted along beside her, but even they knew to stay clear. She hoped she could slip the food into the young bull's feeding trough and get away fast, but he spotted her approach, his eyes red with anger. "Please be nice to me today," she said, tipping the bucket as quickly as possible. Herkimer butted at her with his stubby horns, and half the grain ended up in the dirt. "You should be nice to the one who brings you food," she said. She lowered the rake to begin a little cleanup. Hopefully he'd be distracted and stay still while he was munching.

Herkimer, however, had different plans. He lashed out like a student in a kickboxing class, knocking Luanne to the ground right atop one of his piles. She shot up and stumbled out of the way. "I tried," she said, using a stick to brush off her backside. "You're on your own now!"

She loved all animals, big and small, but had a healthy respect for ones with hooves. Now, hooves or no hooves, the goats needed milking. She approached the three with an encouraging smile. "Good morning, Flower." The first goat lifted her head and walked up to the milking stand without prompting. She even seemed agreeable when Luanne set the bucket on the stand and gently tugged a teat. A stream of milk splattered into the bucket. But as Luanne pulled again, Flower kicked the bucket and spilled the milk.

After getting the same uncooperative results from Thumper and Bambi, Luanne wearily attended to the rest of the animals. She paused at the edge of the garden. "I think you got carried away," she'd told Henry the day he'd tilled the land. The idea of growing vegetables had excited him so much that he'd prepared nearly an acre. Henry'd spent hours tilling and weeding. There was nothing they wouldn't try to grow. One time they went to the general store to buy some gardening supplies and she'd wandered off to another section. When she returned, Henry was at the cashier, checking out with a great pile of seed envelopes: one of every kind they had in stock. They grew asparagus, peas, potatoes, beets, carrots, cucumbers, peppers, corn, tomatoes, squash, and even some vegetables she'd never heard of before. Henry was an expert at preparing and cooking vegetables with meals. But the garden would have to wait, at least for now.

Before she could rest, she needed to complete one more chore. The well had gone dry again. She could get some water in town for herself but the animals needed more, every day, and the best way to accomplish that was collecting water from the stream.

She tried to heft the bulky fifty-gallon barrel by the side of the house. It was heavier than she remembered. She struggled to get it onto the little trailer behind the garden tractor. She rarely drove the tractor. It was Henry's toy. To her, it felt awkward to control, especially on the rugged inclines and ditches of their land. But the animals needed water. She swung her leg over, took a seat, and started the ignition. "Stay here," she told Topper and Chief.

The powerful orange tractor lurched. "Whoa!" she said. She rode the brake all the way down the bumpy driveway. "Outta the way," she warned the chickens. "I'll be right back!" she called to the sheep in the field.

When it came time to turn onto the main road, she hesitated. Traffic was rarely a problem there—in fact, there had been times they'd gone a whole day without seeing another vehicle drive past their house—but there was no shoulder. If a car came up fast behind her slow-moving tractor, she'd have no place to pull over. She hesitated, looked both ways, and then eased the tractor onto the dirt road, as far to the side as she could manage. She prayed that she wouldn't fall in a ditch. She looked straight ahead, willing the tractor to keep on course.

The distance down the road to the stream had never seemed so far before. She parked on the edge where a level patch of grass stretched beside a small bridge. She had to lean over the bridge railing, lower a pail with a rope, and haul the pail back up. Then she returned to the tractor and dumped the water in the barrel. After she'd tipped in dozens of buckets, she worried that the weight of the water would be too heavy and would cause the tractor to rear up. She certainly didn't want to fall off and have the tractor and the barrel of water fall on top of her. It was only half full, but she didn't dare fill it any higher.

She climbed back onto the tractor and drove slowly back home. "Don't tip over, don't tip over," she whispered. Then, when she hit a bump, louder: "Don't tip over!" She reached across and patted the hood. "You can do it. Atta girl. A little farther now." She didn't think it was possible to drive a tractor any slower than she was at the moment. Her arms shook as she gripped the wheel. *I've got to get back to the animals.* She inched down the road. The last incline approached; the hill just before their driveway. She thought of getting out and pushing the machinery from behind, but the image of losing her grip and having everything come crashing down upon her squelched that idea.

At last the tractor crawled to the top of the hill and she turned into the driveway. The sheep and goats bleated. She got out and filled their troughs with water. The sun beat down on her shoulders. It was past midday already. As she dipped the bucket into the barrel again, it scraped the bottom. She sighed, climbed back onto the tractor, eased it back onto the main road and did it all over again.

When she dragged herself into the house again, she noticed her empty coffee cup. She hadn't eaten all day. No wonder she was hungry. She heated up some leftovers and carried a plate out onto the porch and sunk onto a chair. *"Lord, get me through another day."*

Topper and Chief sat at her feet, hoping for handouts. She tried not to worry about Henry, or how she would manage the farm alone, but she still had no idea. When exhaustion finally took over, she fell asleep in her chair. She awakened to a strange swishing sound. Gentle, peaceful. The sky was dark, except for a full, round moon. The swooshes directed her gaze down to the pond, which shone in the glow of the exquisite moon. She raised her head. Ducks, about twenty of them, lined the width of the pond. Together they dove, each one breaking the surface tension gently as an Olympian swimmer with a sleek rip entry. With only a ripple they rose again. The moonlight illuminated a million sparkles against their feathers. Never before had she seen the ducks perform such a maneuver. They moved with such harmony, such serenity. It was as if they were sending a message especially for her. Her heart rate slowed and she began to feel weightless, floating over the scene. She tried not to move a muscle, not wanting to break the spell. Repeatedly, the ducks dove and rose, gliding elegantly all the way to the end of the pond. Then they turned and paddled back the other way, in perfect unison.

Little Lorrie grows strong enough to stand alone.

Henry stops to hug his friend Gertie.

Corky and Luanne take good care of a rabbit.

Hay and grain to munch make for contented goats.

The pond reflects a tranquil mood.

Animals Love

Chapter 14

Stand by Me

THE COOP DOOR opened with a creak and the chickens all spilled out, chattering like a cluster of schoolgirls gossiping after class. "Good morning, Henny. Good morning, Penny," she said as they hurried by. She scattered corn and filled the water bowls. Picking up her basket, she felt through the hay in the nest boxes to gather the eggs. Usually she found about eighteen eggs each day, many double yolkers. Her hens were good layers. One time, a white hen had laid an egg so big, it looked like a goose egg. She gave some eggs to friends and family and sold some to the general store in town. It made her feel good to raise animals that provided sustenance to others.

Next she made her rounds of the animals in the barn and pastures, feeding, cleaning out stalls, spreading hay. She stroked and patted as many animals as she could while she worked; a hug, a rub, or just a touch as she went by. Even those raised for food, she believed, deserved more than just humane treatment, but loving care. "My, what a nice egg!" she said to a chicken. "You're a good boy, aren't you?" she told Arthur, the ram.

When it was time to feed the young bull, she hummed softly. As she drew closer, she broke into song. "Herkimer loves me, yes I know," she sang. He didn't exactly fall for it, but she was able to get away before any incident.

Down in the lower pasture, the goats munched their food. She led Flower up to the milking stand first. When the trough was empty, she started to kick. Luanne shrieked, grabbed the bucket, and saved it before it tipped over. "Okay, you win," she laughed. She got up and refilled the trough. The goats all stood still for milking just as long as there was food to eat.

She finished all the chores quickly, bustled inside and got showered and changed. That day was to be her first visit with Henry. In the beginning of treatment he wasn't allowed communication with anyone, but now he had earned privileges. She packed a bag with a few supplies Henry had requested and climbed into her car. It had been running sluggish and the oil light was on, so she stopped at the general store and bought a few quarts of oil and threw them in the trunk. She drove two hours to the hospital/rehab center in St. Johnsbury, stopping at the gas station nearby where she arranged to have them change the oil. She said she'd pick up the car when she was done.

Henry looked tired and pale, and his eyes heavy. He wore a blue T-shirt and jeans, and had stubble on his face. She couldn't even imagine how exhausting it must be to battle those demons, to come face to face with what was killing him and say he was not going to do that anymore.

She greeted him with a big smile and a hug. "How's it going?" Luanne settled into a wing chair in the living-room-like lobby.

"I'm coming along." Henry rarely had a lot to say, especially about emotions. He looked around awkwardly.

They talked about the farm. She updated him on all the animals and assured him that she was getting along fine. "Except for Herkimer," she said. "He's ornery."

"Kinda like me," Henry laughed. It was good to see him laugh.

"So what are your days like here? What do you do?"

"We have therapy sessions. Group sessions. Classes. Last night we went bowling."

"Are you getting better?" she asked earnestly.

Henry nodded. "I am. I'm starting to feel better." Then the emotions came spilling out. "You know what's sad? So many of the kids, they're so young. Too young to be in here. And they don't have anyone. They say they've been disowned or rejected, and no one ever comes to see or support them. They say that those who have a loved one standing with them have

226

a better chance of recovery." He rubbed his stubbly chin. "Thank you for standing with me."

"Of course," she said hugging him and not letting go. "Why wouldn't I?"

"You didn't ask for this."

She looked into his eyes. "I'm not perfect either. We're in this together. Don't you forget that."

When the visit was over she felt a seed of hope sprout in her heart. She walked to the garage to pick up her car. The mechanic wiped his hand on his coveralls when he saw her. "I'm sorry," he said, "but we can't let you have that car back."

"Why not?"

"It's unsafe to drive. The tie rod is just hanging by a thread. We can fix it up, but I can't guarantee we can get to it today."

Luanne called Uncle Ward. "Is a tie rod important?" she asked.

"I'll say. It's what helps you steer the car."

"Is it safe to drive home?"

"Wouldn't recommend it."

She didn't have any money to pay for repairs, and she had to get home to the animals. Eventually she convinced the mechanic to let her take the car, promising to bring it to her own garage immediately.

When she arrived home, she stopped at the garage in town. The worker there put the car up on the lift. "How far did you just come?" he asked. "You must have had an angel riding with you." The entire tie rod assembly fell off in his hands.

TRUST

The rabbit should have been named Angel because he was pure white with fluffy fur that puffed on the sides like wings. But Luanne's kids had named him Tibbar, which, they explained, was backwards for rabbit. No matter the name, it was the rabbit she saw hopping down the hall first. What came next caused her to do a double-take.

She was in her bedroom picking up clothes and tossing them into a laundry basket. Her two older kids were home from junior high school and Randy had just gotten off the bus from elementary school. The kids collected animals. Since the divorce, she saw no need to limit the number of pets anymore. Whenever a class hamster needed to be kept over vacation, her kids volunteered. If a friend's cat had kittens, they found a way to bring one home. At the moment the menagerie consisted of a turtle, two guinea pigs, a rabbit, a cat and a dog.

Her bedroom door was open and she looked out into the hall. The kids sometimes let Tibbar out of his cage to get some exercise, but usually outside and under supervision. Now Tibbar hopped down the hall unattended, white ears flopping to the sides. Next came Nemo, the seal gray cat, padding softly after the rabbit. Following the cat was curly-haired Corky, bouncing with youthful friskiness.

Luanne had never seen the animals loose all together like that, and certainly not in hot pursuit. She wondered if this was a game or a chase. She dropped the laundry basket and caught up to the madcap parade.

When she rounded the corner into the living room, there were the animals. Tibbar crouched on the rug, nose twitching. Nemo lay beside him, casually licking his paw. Then Corky sprawled behind them as if wrapping them with his limbs. The three rested together in complete trust and peace. As Luanne watched, mesmerized, a passage from Isaiah came to her mind: the wolf would lie down with the lamb, the leopard with the goat, the calf and the lion and the yearling together. Despite the divorce, raising the kids on her own, struggling with finances, trying to make it day by day, she felt a promise wash over her. God would bring peace to the world; God would bring peace to her life.

Chapter 15

Bountiful Harvest

S HE'D BEEN WATCHING the corn all summer; from tiny green shoots to tall, lean stalks, taller than herself. The tassels had turned a beautiful golden blond. But there, in front of her, the rows looked like they'd been run over by a train. Today of all days! After thirty days, Henry was coming home from rehab. How would he think she'd taken care of his garden? Luanne hadn't had time to give it much attention.

She bent down and studied the dirt. Tiny raccoon footprints. They must have had a feast, ravaging the plants and leaving barely

231

an ear uneaten. How she'd wanted corn for Henry's welcome home dinner. Fortunately, with a garden so big, there were many other options.

They sat down to the meal of roasted pork, steamed beet greens and roasted potatoes. Henry's red T-shirt hung as if he'd lost weight while he was away, but his skin glowed and he moved with a new energy. He looked even younger than when they'd first met. His eyes sparkled. "Missed this," he said, raising his fork.

"They must not have fed you well there." Luanne smiled.

"Not like this."

She knew there was still a journey ahead. She'd disposed of every bottle of beer and found every liquor bottle hidden around the house—some outside in the pigpen, even— and poured them down the drain. He'd have to attend AA meetings and stay away from Tom and his other drinking buddies. But ever since they'd found those little folded booklets in the stacks of newspapers, they began to develop a new understanding that God was helping them. At church nobody asked where

Henry had been. "We've been praying for you," was all they said, and they accepted him back without question.

Before climbing up to the loft for bed that night, Henry kissed her gently. "I won't let you down," he said.

She melted into his arms. Those were words she'd never heard from anyone before. *I won't let you down.* What powerful words. She'd said those same words repeatedly, to strays, to animals who were sick and injured. She'd felt that sentiment in return, as they ministered to her heart. But those were animals. It felt new, and a bit astounding, to hear that from another person.

In the morning, the chores beckoned as usual, and Henry happily set to work. Luanne pulled on some heavy gloves to help him mend the fence. Topper and Chief ran along, followed by Lorrie. The little lamb thought she was a dog. The cooler weather made Lorrie frisky and she kicked up her heels. The dogs chased after her. Watching the three play, Luanne felt light and free. She searched for breaks in the fence while Henry pounded nails into posts to support damaged chicken wire.

"What's this?" Luanne asked. She bent to pick up a white tube, a section of water pipe. "This doesn't look like anything of ours."

"Don't recognize it," Henry said.

A little way farther along the fence, she found a screwdriver. "Is this yours, Henry?" she asked.

"Nope. I don't have one with a handle like that," he answered.

"Strange. I doubt anyone's come over to work on our land while we're not looking!"

"Can't imagine where that came from."

They worked on the fence, repairing the wire foot by foot. Near the back edge, Luanne found yet another strange object hidden in the grass: an insulated lunch bag. This time there were telltale teeth marks along the edges. Of course, the bag was empty. She knew the culprits immediately.

"Topper! Chief! What have you been up to?" she scolded. The two dogs looked away guiltily.

Later, she determined that the stolen items were coming from construction workers who were building a house up the road. The dogs must have run through the fields and helped themselves. When she returned the items, the workers laughed and told her it was okay. They'd been enjoying the dogs' visits and had never even missed the miscellaneous objects.

"But your lunch!" Luanne said. She handed them a basket of home-baked muffins and jelly, hoping it would make up for things.

One of the biggest jobs before them was the garden. They'd planted everything from asparagus to zucchini. After endless hours tilling, hoeing, and weeding, the garden flourished—row after row of deep forest green, spring green, olive green, and vibrant jungle green. Tall stalks, bushy leaves, tendrils winding up wooden stakes. Melons of yellow, gold, and orange. At this time of year much of the garden was fruitful; now all they seemed to lack was enough time to bring in the harvest.

"The wheelbarrow has a flat!" Luanne said, trying to maneuver it over a clump of grass.

"I'll push it." Henry took over the handles. "Oh, and I just took a phone call—they're coming to dig the well tomorrow." After hearing about her adventures collecting water, Henry insisted it was time to get a new well drilled.

"But where are we going to get the money?" Luanne had asked.

Henry wasn't sure either. "We'll just have to find a way."

The drilling rig arrived after sunup. The powerful truck with a folded contraption on the back lumbered up the driveway, awakening the dogs, chickens, and every other creature. Luanne and Henry threw on their jackets and ran out the door.

Two men with baseball caps and leather gloves set to work determining the proper drilling location, bracing the tires and securing the derrick. A tall shaft rose from the back of the truck amid a metal arrangement of drums and wires. The setup was meticulously slow until, finally, the motor kicked up, earsplittingly loud. Topper and Chief ran off and hid in the woods.

"Hoist the drill string," one man called.

The drill string didn't look like a string at all, but an assemblage of pipes and collars and machinery. A traveling block pulled the wires up and raised the drill. When the drill bit flew down, it hit the earth with a shattering clang. It squeaked up and boomed down, sending dirt billowing.

Luanne busied herself cleaning the barn, but every few minutes she poked around to check on progress. "Any water yet?" she yelled over the crashes.

The men shook their heads. "We're using the last extension," one hollered.

Luanne steadied herself against the barn door. She had hoped they'd hit water sooner. The work would be charged by the foot. The deeper the well, the greater the expense. Already the cost of the well would be a struggle, but now the bill would be even higher than they'd anticipated. Luanne felt weary of things being a struggle. Building a roof over their heads had taken years, and still the house wasn't complete. Even the animals she loved so much were a constant worry. She was tired. She rested her head in her hands and closed her eyes. *How can I do this? How can I do this?* In the stillness of the barn, she felt God telling her, *"Trust Me."*

By the time the sun began to sink behind the distant mountains and the sky seemed painted with gentle pinks, the workers let out a cheer. Luanne and Henry ran out to see.

"Four hundred-eighty feet!" they said, wiping their brows.

Luanne and Henry embraced. They'd hit water. Beautiful, clear, life-sustaining water.

She clutched the bill for the well in her hands as she stood in line at the bank. She hadn't planned on the total being so high. Although the drillers expected the bill paid in full, all she could offer was a partial payment.

"I'd like to keep my account open," she pushed her bank book through the window to the teller, "but withdraw all my money. Four hundred dollars."

The teller looked up her account. "Do you mean four thousand dollars?"

Luanne laughed at the implausibility. "No. I only have four hundred dollars in my account. Look, see?" she pointed at the numbers in the bankbook.

"Yes, ma'am," the teller nodded. "But our records show this." She read a number and ran through some files.

"How could that be?" Luanne asked.

"The new amount seems to be due to an insurance check."

"I don't know anything about any insurance check. Where did it come from?"

"I don't know. But it all seems to be in order. The money's yours."

The teller counted the money into Luanne's hands. Four thousand, eight hundred and twenty-six dollars. Her heart pounded.

Exactly the amount of the well-drilling bill.

Luanne stood at the well, the dirt still loose and rich around it. Nothing but a metal pipe, capped over. Nearly flush with the ground, insignificant in appearance, critical in function. Deeper than she could picture, hundreds of feet beneath her feet, spilling forth with the most pure, vital substance for all life.

A bead of sunlight showered down on the fields. It was a time of transition. That morning frost had gently adorned the pastures. Before long the grass would die and then be covered by snow. How amazing that, despite the pounding from brutal weather, it sprang up again each year, green and vibrant and strong! She thought back to her homes, her struggles, her heartbreaks. It was true: Something seemingly weak and insignificant could become strong and thrive.

"I've got the vegetables!" Henry plodded up from the garden, pushing the wheelbarrow with the rickety wheel. Topper and Chief pranced behind him, followed by frolicking Lorrie. "Think I've got enough?" he asked.

Luanne laughed joyously. The wheelbarrow was heaped with green, yellow, and orange leaves, gourds, and roots. Their bounty overflowed. Later that day, friends and family would be arriving for a feast. Turkey. Potatoes, carrots, squash, and peas from the garden. Everything they'd grown or raised on their own. God had provided abundantly.

"I'm going to get cooking," Henry said. "Are you coming in?"

"In a bit," she answered. "There's something I need to do first."

She pulled on a heavy pair of work gloves, and the animals followed her to the side of the house facing the pond. There she'd started a flower garden. Phlox and marigolds mixed with wild cornflower and Queen Anne's lace. For all her efforts, though, most of the flowers got trampled, flooded, or eaten by goats. The one plant that remained, smack in the center, was a large bull thistle. All summer, its huge pink flowers had brightened the hillside. "You don't want that thing," friends would say when they came to visit. "It'll spread like wildfire. It will choke out all the other plants."

It may have been just a weed, but oh, that brilliant pink! Bright yellow finches visited its flowers. Monarch butterflies came to feed of its nectar. "It's the best thing blooming in my garden," Luanne always countered.

That day, the pink flowers had turned to seed, a soft fuzz like a dandelion. Luanne knelt humbly beside the plant. It was pretty, but its spiny leaves stuck to the animals' fur, and she was forever pulling its thorns off her clothes. Before company came for dinner, she would pull that weed out of the garden.

She reached down to where the stem met the earth. A breeze picked up and sent the seeds soaring, feathery parachutes as delicate as snow. Some floated all the way down to the pond with its dazzling goldfish. The pond, which glistened with ice and snow in the winter. Which sparkled in the moonlight. And, which gently embraced the ducks as they sent her encouraging messages of hope.

Other seeds lifted up toward the mountains and their stunning display. The hills burst with vivid colors created by the master painter. Orange leaves dominated with a flamboyant energy demanding of attention. Near a peak shimmered a small but dazzling patch of gold, the color of the heavens. That magnificent view, that view that first attracted her to the land, never let her down.

The last seed settled in the fleece of the little lamb. "Maaaa!" Lorrie called, wagging her stubby tail. What a blessing to be so completely accepted by gentle little Lorrie. Luanne drew her close. She was grateful that she'd been able to help bring animals into the world and care for them when they were weak. Lorrie nestled against her leg.

At times she was as needy as the little lamb. But, just maybe, she was also as resilient. After all, she had endured storms and setbacks. She reached her free hand out to Topper and Chief. And could it be that she was as accepting as them, and Corky, and the stray dog, Happy? If she thought about it, she was even as strong as the horse at the orphanage and the moor pony in the movie she'd watched as a child. She'd run the farm alone when Henry was in the hospital.

And then, she knew the great secret. God had made her strong and capable and worthy. All the traits she'd admired in the animals all her life, all the gifts they offered—yes!—she possessed those qualities too. Even though she didn't deserve it, she was both nurturing and nurtured, loving and loved.

She rubbed Lorrie's back as the lamb nibbled a prickly leaf of the plant. The thistle seeds had all blown away. Luanne pulled off her work gloves and stood up, leaving the plant alone. She couldn't wait for spring, when those bright pink flowers would bloom again.

Topper and Chief supervise chores on the farm.

The nearly completed house overlooks a thriving garden.

A relaxing time in the pasture.

A Note from the Editors

We hope you enjoy *Heart to Heart, Hand in Paw*, specially selected by the editors of the Books and Inspirational Media Division of Guideposts, a nonprofit organization. In all of our books, magazines and outreach efforts, we aim to deliver inspiration and encouragement, help you grow in your faith, and celebrate God's love in every aspect of your daily life.

Thank you for making a difference with your purchase of this book, which helps fund our many outreach programs to the military, prisons, hospitals, nursing homes and schools. To learn more, visit GuidepostsFoundation.org.

We also maintain many useful and uplifting online resources. Visit Guideposts.org to read true stories of hope and inspiration, access OurPrayer network, sign up for free newsletters, download free e-books, join our Facebook community, and follow our stimulating blogs.

To learn about other Guideposts publications, including our best-selling devotional *Daily Guideposts*, go to ShopGuideposts.org, call (800) 932-2145 or write to Guideposts, PO Box 5815, Harlan, Iowa 51593.